CHENNAI

Chennai

A city of change

edited by

MALVIKA SINGH

ACADEMIC FOUNDATION
NEW DELHI

www.academicfoundation.com

First published in 2011
by

ACADEMIC FOUNDATION
4772-73 / 23 Bharat Ram Road, (23 Ansari Road),
Darya Ganj, New Delhi - 110 002 (India).
Phones : 23245001 / 02 / 03 / 04.
Fax : +91-11-23245005.
E-mail : books@academicfoundation.com
www.academicfoundation.com

Cataloging in Publication Data--DK
Courtesy: D.K. Agencies (P) Ltd. <docinfo@dkagencies.com>

Chennai : a city of change / edited by Malvika Singh.
p. cm.
ISBN 13: 9788171888856
ISBN 10: 8171888852

1. Madras (India)--History. 2. Madras (India)--Description and travel. I. Singh, Malvika.

DDC 954.82 22

Typeset by Italics India, New Delhi.
Printed and bound in India.

For

PREMA SRINIVASAN

Contents

Introduction

MALVIKA SINGH

The journal SEMINAR turned fifty in the year 2009. At that time we decided to bring out themed 'compendiums' from the vast treasure of material that the monthly had published over the five and more, decades. As part of that ongoing project, Academic Foundation have reproduced six special issues of SEMINAR, as a set of individual books, that celebrate the historic and famed cities of Delhi; Bombay, now Mumbai; Calcutta, now Kolkata; Madras, now Chennai; Hyderabad and Lucknow. We are delighted that this work will be accessible to a wider audience of Indians as well as visitors to India, who would want to share and experience the many special, personal and individual insights into the life and times of these cities, based on memories, on hitherto unspoken behind-the-scenes stories, some full of joy and others that lament the change, all of which are woven together in an extraordinary tapestry.

My gratitude to Rituraj and Sanu Kapila for having recognised the merit of these carefully crafted mini compendiums, and for reproducing them with much care. My thanks to all the writers who participated in the issues of SEMINAR, making them lively, unusual and substantive. To my colleagues at SEMINAR, my sincere thanks for supporting the many SEMINAR related 'ventures' like this one!

A city of change

HARSH SETHI

IN contrast to our other metropolis', Madras/Chennai has most often been presented as an idyllic, genteel city, an example of 'simple living and high thinking'. If Delhi comes across as a court surrounded by villages, its soul corrupted by power, Bombay as a worshipper of mammon and Calcutta as a city more marked by its past than present, Chennai with its unhurried, almost sleepy pace, is seen as representing the continuity of Indian (read Hindu) cultural traditions.

True that the public culture of the North is rarely marked by grace, the Lakhnavi/Mughal *adas* notwithstanding. Our caste appears more casteist, our sectarian strife more intense, and our politicians just that much more crass and rapacious. The usual reference is to Bihar and U.P. Hardly surprising that most commentators believe that the Narmada represents the boundary between civilization and barbarism.

If the cultural difference is not to be traced to the erroneous 'racial' basis of Aryan and Dravidian, do we instead focus on the differential impact of Muslim rule? For many, South Indian culture has preserved, in a more pristine and pure form, the traditional Hindu ways of living. Even granting that such a proposition is implicitly 'communal' and does little to acknowledge the substantial Muslim (and Christian) presence in the states of the South (a common North Indian error), it cannot be denied that unlike the North, the Brahmin in the South enjoys a unique position, a far greater social importance and weight.

To the outsider, the South is Madras, not just the city but the idea – ritually defined, vegetarian and conservative, if not orthodox. Despite the fact that the more important temples – Madurai, Chidambaram, Tirupati, Guruvayur and Annamalai are not in Madras, and nor is it the seat of the Shankaracharya, the city, in popular imagination, represents the power of spirituality and faith.

Like all representations claiming to capture the essence, this one too is mistaken. Starting as the first English outpost on land negotiated from the local rulers, Madras/Chennai has grown into a sprawling metropolis afflicted by all the problems marking large urban agglomerations – overcrowding, decaying infrastructure, impersonality and, above all, a crippling water shortage. When a vast majority of the populace has little access to potable water and even the better-off are forced to rely on bottled water, tension is endemic. More surprising, however, is the fact that the shortages have, so far, not translated into severe water riots.

Much is made about the Madrasi's understated austerity, the absence of garishness in public and private buildings, how even the powerful and famous lead reticent lives, that a M.S. Subbulakshmi answers her own phone and the person next to you in the milk queue could well be a famous scientist. There is the amazing *katcheri* season which attracts hordes of music lovers, many young, and we have *The Hindu*, the one national newspaper still retaining space for serious articles. And of course, the fact that even the non-Hindu communities seem to effortlessly merge into the dominant public culture, the religious distinctions subsumed in a common cultural style. Of all our major cities, Chennai has been least disturbed by Hindu-Muslim conflict.

It is rare, in these accounts foregrounding temples and spirituality, devotional Carnatic music and Bharatnatyam, vegetarian food and Nalli sarees, love for scholarship (who can contest the fact of C. Rajagopalachari as our most erudite politician-statesman) and austerity, the Theosophical Society and Kalakshetra, to examine the role of the non-Brahmin, rationalist movement challenging Brahmin supremacy in public affairs and institutions on the city and the people. Or how an anti-caste movement over time consolidates caste divisions such that we even have clear differences between Brahmin and non-Brahmin Tamil and the rise of caste/region specific political parties whose hold refuses to wither and whose shifting alliances make psephology a hazardous exercise.

Nor does this accommodate the inordinate influence of films and film personalities over politics, popular culture and discourse. Nowhere else can we see a shrine dedicated to MGR, with fur cap and dark glasses, or a temple with actress Khushboo as the presiding deity. And no other part of the country has witnessed suicides and ritual mutilation on news of the death of an Annadurai or MGR. The hold of fan clubs on politics and the frenzied adulation of stars cannot but affect civic culture. It thus causes little comment when politicians in power, in true filmy style, expend more energy to harass their rivals (though Punjab now seems to be making the grade) than ensure good governance.

A major enigma is the status of women. Like Mumbai and Kolkata and unlike Delhi, Chennai enjoys a well-deserved reputation for women's safety. A ride in the city's efficient bus system shows little sign of eve-teasing and seats reserved for women are never commandeered by men. But indices of domestic violence are high, and across class divides, demonstrating the gulf between public perception and private reality. The same remains true of Dalits who, despite the social justice plank of the Dravida movement, are subjected to endemic social exclusion and violence.

Old timers lament the passing away of the good old days – be it of Hindu greatness or British fair play. Madras, after all, was the first

English outpost, the site of the initial experimentation with rules and regulations, libraries and archives, the municipal corporation, modern banking and even the Indian army. Even as the action shifted to Calcutta and Bombay and then Delhi, Madras retained its importance in national affairs – from the founding of the Congress to Gandhiji's call for *swarajya*. It refused to be relegated to the outposts of the empire.

With all its continuities, Madras/Chennai today is a different city. The Brahmins may no longer dominate public affairs (this despite Chief Minister Jayalalithaa being an Iyengar), but they are crucial to the private sector. Having been forced out of their traditional environs and occupations by a combination of reservations and the non-Brahmin movement, they have become a pan-Indian, even global, community which retains an interest in the city, dominating industry and trade.

As it struggles to define a new identity for itself seeking to outgrow the traditional confines, partly as a result of pressure from the young, present Chennai now approximates any other large city. The tempo is undoubtedly faster as is the new importance to flash, display and consumer choice. Be it clothes, music, cuisine or nightlife – Chennai is no sleepy town, possibly no match for a Mumbai or Bangalore, but offering sufficient diversity.

There is also the grime and the decay, fraying infrastructure and an underlying edge of tension. Nevertheless, there is also the tradition of public service, be it the K.S. Sanjivi initiated Voluntary Health Scheme or the Shankar Netralaya which ensure quality health care at low cost for the less privileged. The state's rulers take justifiable pride in their mid-day meal scheme and primary health centres. And business, probably more than elsewhere, follows a code of ethics foregrounding substance over form.

Chennai/Madras is a complex, contradictory city experiencing the pangs of transformation. This volume introduces the Queen of the Coromandel, the Gateway to the South, a city responsible for many innovations, which will hopefully extend its glorious past into the future.

First city of modern India

S. MUTHIAH

MADRAS that is Chennai, the Queen of the Coromandel, is a comparatively new city, less than 400 years old. During its first 150 years, however, it was the Gateway of India. Today, the first city of modern India is India's fourth largest and the Gateway to the South.

Over the centuries Nestorian merchants and Arab navigators, Greek philosophers and Roman centurions, 'Portugee' hidalgos and Dutch burghers, English East Indiaman and French musketeers, even Danish sailors and German scholars descended on Coromandel's ancient shores in search of diamonds and pearls, ivory and sandalwood, cordage and sails and, above all, the finest cottons in the world.

These were the riches of a great hinterland where for centuries ancient kingdoms had risen and fallen and risen again. To the South lay the maritime Pandya and Chola kingdoms, possessors of an amazing artistic legacy. To the West were the Pallavas, who had absorbed the skills of the Chalukyas and the Hoysalas and sculpted veritable open air museums. To the North were the last vestiges of Vijayanagar and the southernmost outposts of the Mughals. Their nayaks and nawabs added the final touches to the endless wealth of art, craft and skill that thrived in Coromandel's hinterland.

To Coromandel's shores, following the trade routes first navigated by the Arabs, then centuries later by the Portuguese and Dutch, the British came in the early 17th century. Seeking a permanent trading settlement and investment in a textile-producing area, Andrew Cogan, the chief agent of the East India Company at Machilipatnam, sent his Factor at Armagon near Nellore, Francis Day, scouting for a place where the Company, established on the first day of 1600, could find 'cloath better cheape'.

That he'd found it was what Day reported in July 1639, explaining too the land grant that his *dubash* Beri Thimappa had negotiated. England on that July day was richer by a strip of 'no man's sand' three miles long, one mile wide at its broadest, protected by the surf-wracked waters of the Bay of Bengal on its east, an estuary in the south and a river to its west. All it needed was a thorn hedge to its north to protect it.

This would be England's main settlement on India's east coast, Cogan determined, and within a year he had established a factory, in effect a stockade enclosing a warehouse and a few homes. On 23rd April 1640, St. George's Day, they grandiosely called it Fort St. George, the heart of what they named Madraspatnam after the neighbouring fishing villages that the Madra (Madeiros) family of San Thomé owned. To its north, along the bank of the west river, Thimappa settled weavers and dyers, bleachers and washers he had brought in from the land of the Telugus and they named their settlement Chennapatnam after the father of the Nayak whose largesse to the East India Company had given them a new home and the security of assured business.

Around the two towns, the Madras that is Chennai grew, taking in declining ancient settlements with histories more than 2000 years old. The Company's Governor and his Council in Madras were, from the 1640s till 1772, in charge of all English East India Company settlements from Surat to Bantam in Java. It was no wonder, therefore, that the foundations of modern India were laid in Madras, which during this Age of Trade truly became the Gateway to India.

The rest of India may have long forgotten the contribution Madras has made over the years to the development of 'modern India'. Sadly, however, even its own citizens rarely remember their city's contribution to that India, and Madras remains not only a forgotten city but also a 'City of Neglect'.

In Fort St. George we have the genesis of many a facility that subsequently grew into a nation-wide system. It was here that Streynsham Master and William Langhorne and 'Pirate' Pitt who gave England two prime ministers, codified rules and regulations for the new settlement and introduced record keeping – one strand that grew into red tape, and the other into archives. It was here, in the Church of St. Mary's in the Fort – the first church built by the British in India – that the country's first orphanage and western-style school were established; today, they have both grown and are thriving. St. George's School set the pattern for education, private as well as state-sponsored. Also, St. Mary's established a library that was to evolve into the present library system. And the banking facilities first established here went through various *avatars* before becoming the State Bank of India.

It was in this Fort that Governor Elihu Yale set up the first western-style hospital in India, primitive though it was. Outside its walls, he inaugurated the first municipal corporation in the country. The Survey School started here was to grow into Guindy Engineering College, the oldest technical training institution outside of Europe. And it was here that the Indo-Saracenic architectural form was first introduced in the country.

Until Calcutta became the Company's headquarters in the late 18th century, Madras cast the seeds for much that has influenced India's present. It was here that Job Charnock was equipped for the mission that culminated in the founding of Calcutta; Stringer Lawrence lay the foundation of the Indian Army in Fort St. David and Fort St. George, Cuddalore and Madras with the Madras Regiment;

Clive and that army played their part at Plassey; the first revolts against the British were in Madurai and Vellore by those from that army, and there was much more as the years rolled by.

There were no dreams of empire among these hardy traders, each intent on turning a quicker penny for himself rather than the Company and looking forward to going back 'Home' and settling down to the life of a 'Nabob'. The dreams of empire were initially those of Jean Francois Dupleix, who governed French Pondicherry, and his 'Begum' Jeanne. When he seized Fort St. George in 1746, it was to allow him a free hand to play the great game of protection that would help France bring local rulers to tribute-paying heel. When Fort St. George was rendered to the East India Company in 1749, the English demonstrated they had learnt their French lessons well. Over the next two decades, they ended the French dream and sowed the seeds of the Raj, having first prepared the ground during an Age of Expansionism that operated through the use of mercenaries.

With the French no longer a power in India by the 1760s, and the Mughals in decline, the English became the dominant influence. With the Company's new army ensuring peace, the English moved out of forts to build homes and the symbols of the Establishment. In Madras, throughout the 18th century, such building took the form of the Regency, the Georgian and the Gothic – army engineers building in the styles they remembered from 'home' and the books of Roman and Greek architecture they pored over.

Their large airy public buildings, uniformly lime-washed a white that gleamed in the sun, were in striking contrast to the palaces and forts of the local princely orders. The homes of the new zamindari – prosperous British merchants and traders – followed the same architectural style, but surrounding themselves as they did with gardens around the houses and tree-rich 'parks' beyond, they made Madras famous for its 'garden houses'. Expansive living and extensive entertaining became the lifestyle of Madras in its second age – a sign of architectural things to come.

As forgotten today as Cogan, Day and Thimappa, not only in India but in Madras as well, is Chepauk Palace, built under the protective guns of Fort St. George as the home of the Nawabs of the Carnatic. Today, Indo-Saracenic is described as architectural form most favoured by the British, developed to depict their regal public face, and the princely order aped it to convey a similar impression. The high noon of this form of architecture was Lutyens' and Baker's New Delhi, though they fought shy of the term used to describe Mant's and Chisholm's, Irwin's and Jacob's masterpieces. Few remember that its beginnings were in the palace the first Nawab of the Carnatic, Mohamed Ali of Wallajah, wanted built in the Fort and then agreed to on a site across the river from its glacis.

He also accepted the services of Company engineer, later Company contractor, Paul Benfield to design and build the first British vision of a Hindu and Muslim architectural amalgam. The man responsible for the walls of the Fort and the town walls was an honest engineer who built to last, but he was also a shrewd exploiter of opportunity. And when the Nawab could not pay his bills, he continued to lead the hungry pack that had lent prodigiously to fuel Mohamed Ali's extravagances.

In the end, the scandal of the Carnatic Debts became one of the most heated debates in the House of Parliament before settlement was reached: the British government would settle on the debtor's behalf what it considered the legitimate claims of the creditors – and even those ran into millions of pounds (in the 18th century). In turn, it would accept the Carnatic – the Coromandel and its hinterland from Kanyakumari to the southern districts of Orissa – from the Nawab whose accession they had backed and for which they had fought the French in the Carnatic wars. The empire had begun.

With the fall of the Company and the dawn of the Age of Empire after 1857, the Queen of the Coromandel began to enjoy its finest hour, developing as a spacious and gracious city where commerce was not rushed and seemed civilized, and art and culture and the good life flourished. Late 19th century Madras was to contribute much to the

India of today, while the 50 years till World War II were to change the city's own skyline.

It was men of the Madras Army like Colin Mackenzie, William Lambton and Francis Buchanan who were responsible for the opening up of India and discovering its wealth. Mackenzie's land surveys and his Indological obsession, Lambton's Great Trigonometrical Survey from Cape Comorin to Nagpur and which George Everest extended to the high Himalaya, and Dr. Buchanan's findings of the immense wealth the land offered – all led to the creation of the Survey of India, the Archaeological Survey of India, the Zoological Survey of India and the Botanical Survey of India.

Charles Trevelyan's role in establishing the Indian Civil Service and his dialogues with brother-in-law Macaulay laid the foundations for the systems of education and jurisprudence that we are wedded to today. Thomas Munro's sustained advocacy for greater powers to Indians and much more are not just part of the record but form an integral part of everyday life in India. And in southern India, the opening up of land in its western reaches by men from Madras enabled the development of today's giant plantations that for a century were the driving economic force in this part of the country. These were some of the pioneering steps taken by men of the Madras Presidency.

In more recent times there have been other landmarks. The call for the formation of Congress was first given in Madras, as was the call for *satyagraha* made during Gandhiji's visit to the city. It was here that prohibition was first introduced. It was in Fort St. George that the Justice Party, the first non-Congress government in any part of India, took office. Later, when C.N. Annadurai led the DMK into the legislature in Fort St. George, it was the first time in independent India that a regional party had come into power. It was in Madras that we first heard the call for greater states' rights, which hopefully will one day lead to a reappraisal of the Constitution and a more equitable and federal form of central government. Here too was developed the country's first and biggest industrial estate. And no city in India has a bigger festive music season – or an older one – than Madras.

To serve British soldier and administrator, planter and trader and the investors and investments that kept growing, garden houses for the new settlers, some of the handsomest buildings for the houses of commerce, and palatial public buildings meant to awe with their Indo-Saracenic imperialist aspect were developed by architects and engineers like Robert Chisholm, Henry Irwin, John Goldingham and Norman Pogson, men who also pioneered a college of art, revival of old building methods, the training of engineers and the study of the stars.

The faded splendour of several of the buildings they raised still survives today – the garden houses and palaces of the Raj such as the Senate House, Presidency College, Guindy Engineering, the High Court and the Law College, the General Post Office and the Bank of Madras, the Museum and the Connemara Library, the Art Gallery and the Town Hall.

Perhaps the most significant part of the city, in contrast to other over-crowded areas, is George Town, the Indian settlement that was shifted from its original location north of the Fort to a planned, gridironed square of criss-crossing streets further north. What the city is to London, unprepossessive George Town is to Madras. Both the wholesale trade and the city's private wealth have thrived here from the middle of the 18th century. Both the Indians and the British working here made the Madras to the south of it what it was before World War II, a city of spaciousness and grace, a bastion of conservativeness and courtliness, a commercial centre where the pace of wealth generation allowed for the leisure to enjoy the good life.

World War II changed all that. As the Japanese war machine rolled over East and Southeast Asia, the Allies were left with only two ports in Asia to serve their counter-offensive – Colombo and Madras. It was not merely the soldiers from Britain, North America and Africa and other parts of India who changed Madras. The 'war effort' transformed Madras turning it into a bustling industrial city instead of a quiet trading post that was also a charming laid-back capital. The demands of the war effort attracted thousands of job seekers from the hinterland of the Coromandel, making Madras a 'million' city before the end of the war, more than doubling its population in that fateful decade.

Post independence and Jawaharlal Nehru's vision of an industrialized India, the great trading houses of the Coromandel, which had semi-industrialized during the war, decided to become major industrial conglomerates. Newcomers joined the wartime immigrant population, adding to congestion and creating hovels and tenements. Then, with independence and time, the Presidency disintegrated into various linguistic states. Madras state became Tamil Nadu, but Madras remained its capital. The Queen of the Coromandel was, however, on its way to becoming a metropolis.

Maybe as befitting a metropolis, there is a little less graciousness and a little more rough-and-readiness. But where else in the country is faith greater and more obvious? Or where can you find a year-long cultural season that peaks in December-March with over 2000 concerts, at its climax offering four a day at around a dozen venues for 15 days? Indeed, faith and culture and an unsurpassed variety of southern cuisine, much of it vegetarian, enable Madras to remain closer to a heritage that was ancient when Madras was born. That is the greatest charm of Madras that is Chennai, even as consumerism and 'westernization' take hold.

Indeed, the expressions of faith in Madras are not confined to the garb of pilgrims, the sectarian marks of the faithful or the sacred designs drawn daily in front of houses, big and small. It is most evident in the number of places of worship that abound in the city. Truly a city of a thousand shrines, there is scarcely a street in Madras that does not have its pavement shrine or a towering symbol of someone's faith. Ancient temples, many over ten centuries old, churches built by the Portuguese, the British and the Armenians, mosques where Sunnis and Shias have worshipped for centuries, even Jewish and Chinese cemeteries are all part of the fabric of Madras. Here people show a greater measure of mutual respect for each other's faith, while religion has developed side by side with a rich tradition of religious art and architecture.

In fact, this art and architecture and the crafts of the ages are what combined to inspire men like Benfield and Chisholm, Irwin and Pogson. What they created may, in terms of the Coromandel's historic past, be comparatively new, but without the skills of artisans who worked with lime and mortar, mud and rock, wood and metal, there would not be the buildings and the skyline that made the fort-centred town Day, Cogan and Thimappa founded, the Queen of the Coromandel. Its contribution to the India of today may be forgotten, its memorials to heritage may be under threat, but it remains a city of faith and culture where hope of a still better tomorrow is born afresh every time the sun rises and bathes the Coromandel in hues of fire and gold.

The Madras syndrome

TISHANI DOSHI

A kind of shirt –

Madras: Loosely woven, fine cotton fabric. Vegetable dyed in plaids, stripes and checks. Tends to fade when washed.

'Magical things happen to this shirt when you wash it.'

David Ogilvy

A CITY holds its name like its colour. Madras – Madras – Madras. It swims easily off the tongue. Means everything it says. Believes it can be India's most romantic city because of its pure potential. A port city capable of magic with the second longest strip of beach in the world. And what it can offer is this: the freedom to arrive, explore, drift, dream. A home for illustrious beginnings, meandering middles, infamous endings.

Take away its name and you take away the strings that hold the fabric together. Change its name without its consent and you may as well drown the shirt in hot water, wring it out to dry in the unforgiving sun, and forget all about it. The act in itself is tantamount to allowing a thing of great beauty to fade – allowing an ageing diva to succumb to nostalgia and sing about the good old days when the city had a name you could believe in – when it shone in bright, unweakened colours, and was full of paradox and tradition and fullness. When it balanced the delicate art of revelling in understatement and tooting its own nadaswaram.

1996. Following the feisty footsteps of the Maharashtra government, the city of Madras is renamed so as to put the 'Tamil' back into Tamil Nadu. Madras, they claimed, was not a Tamil name. Why should a capital city be named after a random Portuguese trader, or worse still his wife, whichever version of the story you wish to believe? So, they searched for an alternative. Something more authentic. And this is what they came up with – Chennai. *Nai* – Tamil, for dog. Chennai, a kind of chinny dog. A clunky, ugly word that feels like salt on your teeth and sand in your throat. A heavy name that falls upon the city, choking all its claims to romanticism. A spanner that falls into the works at the crucial time of transformation, as the city hurtles toward the 50-years-after-independence and where-the-hell-are-we mark. A moment in history where people have stopped to take notes. How much more traffic? How many more buildings? How many more people? Choked charm, inert canals, de-fragranced rivers. The second longest strip of beach – 13 km of now adulterated sand.

2003. Following the success of Kerala's tourist campaign, the state launches what it hopes will lift the mantle that has stifled the city. A brand spanking new banner – *Enchanting Tamil Nadu – Experience Yourself,* with Chennai, the capital, as the obvious epicentre. A Seven Point Action Plan which involves unlocking the hidden treasures of the state, positioning Chennai and Coimbatore as destinations for international conferences, as 'India's eastern gateway to the world.' Grabbing those global tourists (of which Madras receives fourth highest in all India), taking them by the hand to the new-improved, cleaned-up Mamallapuram (avatar of the previous Mahabalipuram) and onward to the purportedly plentiful, barely-breathed about gems scattered around the state, pocketing bits of euros and dollars along the way, and funnelling them back into the infrastructure. Severe repositioning. At least, that's the plan.

No mention of the fact that it was much easier to sell when people had a name they could identify with: Madras curry, Madras handkerchiefs, Madras filter coffee, Madras silks, Madras mallipu, Mylapore mamis, Medical missions, mridangams, MGR.

A name 350-years-old in the imagination. A name lighthouses have favoured as ships came in to shore. 1883, Joseph Conrad passes through on the 'Riversdale' and later joins the 'Narcissus' at Bombay (sorry, Mumbai), which later forms material for the novel, *The Nigger of the Narcissus.* Later that same century, Jane Austen's spinster cousin, Philadelphia, passes through as part of the brood of 'good English women', proceeds to have an affair with Warren Hastings, produces a daughter, returns to England and marries Jane's brother. None of this material is apparent in any of Ms. Austen's novels. 1878, the mystical Madam Blavatsky and Colonel Olcott pass through to set up the headquarters of the Madras Theosophical Society. Early 1900s, 40-year-old George Sydney Arundale arrives to head Annie Besant's school of Theosophy, falls in love with the then 16-year-old Rukmani Nilakanta Sastri (later, Rukmani Devi Arundale, later, *Atthai*), marries her despite opposition, stands back to watch the unfolding of an exquisite dancer. 1930s, Somerset Maugham passes through Madras, moves on to Thiruvannamalai (the name stands) to meet Ramana Maharishi who becomes the 'holy man' in *The Razor's Edge.*

A city of illustrious beginnings; birthplace of famous babies who later found other homes – William Makepeace Thackeray, Arnold George Dorsey (later renamed Engelbert Humperdink, in an effort to kick-start his singing career), former England cricket captain, Nasser Hussain. A breeding ground for scientists, mathematicians, physicists of good Tam-Bram stock, and others (John Henry Whitehead). A city of firsts – site of the East India Company's first settlement, place where the apostle Thomas first stepped, from where Christianity spread its wings, first place in the world where payments were made for undergoing a vasectomy (Rs 30 a pop).

A city of meandering middles. Artists, philosophers, yoga gurus, dancers, singers, musicians. Jiddu Krishnamurti fleeting in and out, giving talks under the famous banyan tree. The mathematical genius, Ramanujan, who sailed away to England to work on algebra of inequalities, elliptic functions, continued fractions, partial sums and products of hypergeometric series, but came back to Madras to die of tuberculosis. R.K. Narayan, chronicler of small-town life in South India, making its subtleties available to the world.

Infamous endings: Rajiv Gandhi.

A city, in other words, of incredible comings and goings, but fallible, nonetheless. Because here's the unearthed fact – Chennappa Naicker, Rajah of Chandragiri, who granted the British the right to trade on the coast, the major inspiration for the city's new name, turned out to have faulty origins. Turns out he was a Telugu speaker from Andhra Pradesh. Close, but not close enough.

I still like the alternative theory to the Portuguese coinage – that the city was named after a local fisherman, Madarasan. Improbable, but Tamil enough, romantic at least, and in keeping with the image of the city.

Here's an image of the city. Madras after monsoon rains wears its skies like a Kanchivaram saree: brilliant red, pink, purple, alchemised with those exalted elements of carbon emission, dust, debris, and omnipresent humidity, to create sunscapes of world calibre. A good place to catch one of the few uninterrupted views of the sky in the city is the Adyar Bridge. After crossing it, you can only catch glimpses of orange shards between the towering political cutouts, billboards and buildings. But December in Madras *is* a magical time. The trees are greener, early morning walkers semi-surface in their monkey caps and shawls, young people saunter about in jeans and long-sleeves without breaking into sweat. Even the cows and dogs want to leave their usual shady spots and congregate in the middle of the eternally dug-up roads.

This year, unfortunately, the rains duped us. She teased, taunted, lifted up her silken skirts, skittered about and left the entire state of

Tamil Nadu in a dire state of emergency. Despite a massive rainwater harvesting campaign spearheaded by the Metrowater Board, the failure of the North East monsoon has forced water storage levels to an all time low and has created an uneasy sense of violence born of craving. For a city bordered by the sea, famed for its 'placid and silvery Cooum' (granted, this particular epithet hasn't been true for a while now), these haunting images of water queues, and brightly coloured abandoned plastic water pots, seems surreal, unnatural.

But the problem of water is very real. A recent article in the *Indian Express* quoted the minimum water demand for the city at 180 million litres of water per day for domestic consumption. Now, the amount of hankering involved in the buying, selling, distributing and procuring of these precious litres from the water tankers – the new monsters of the road, who have well-surpassed the PTC buses, is a dangerous affair. By the end of November this year, there had been 120 accidents in Madras involving water tankers (both government and private), 30 deaths and 111 injuries. And these were just road-related accidents!

Even as I write, the death toll continues. An accident reported in this morning's *Hindu* (December 26), described the gruesome crushing to death of a woman and her son by a water tanker, minutes after attending Christmas Mass. Then, take into account the aggression involved off the roads. People are losing lives and body parts (Mr P.K. Palani lost an eye to local thugs who had taken over water distribution in his street), in an effort to exercise their basic rights to available, clean, drinking water.

At the end of it all, there is the same resonance. No groundwater recharge, alternate day water supplies, dwindling reservoirs, salinity, increased water tariffs, serpentine queues. The same sad stories the residents of the city have been living with for years. Except, suddenly, we are on the brink. This was the make or break year. Everyone seems to be talking wells, bores, suppliers, harvesting, neighbourhood villages as alternative water sources (in complete violation of the Water Requirements Act 2002). Looking skyward, asking the prophetic question, *what will we do next year*? Buy gallons of mineral water and bathe our babies in it like the fearful expatriate wives?

Somehow, there seems to be a perpetuation of faith: the idea that *something* will happen. A depression in the bay, a rip in the sky, water tankers that will suddenly behave. Or even more miraculous, a sudden materialization of the chief minister's cross-border visit to negotiate the release of Krishna water. There's an incredible amount of belief.

Meanwhile, the state government has taken over water supply of a different kind.

In November this year, the government-owned Tamil Nadu State Marketing Corporation (TASMAC) took over the wholesale distribution of Indian Made Foreign Liquor (IMFL). This involved putting 8,500 private owners out of business. The government justified this move, saying that it wanted to eliminate the sale of contraband and spurious liquor. This, in the only state which has licensed wine shops but not bars. Now, however, that rule has been relaxed, and liquor shops are allowed to serve the odd peg here and there. A subsequent chain of deaths related to drinking dodgy moonshine has followed.

Perhaps now is the time for retrograde. It being the end of the year and all, with the auspicious Tamil month of *Thai* approaching. January is a time for promises, hopes, wiping clean the slates, an ebb and tide kind of month. The month for marriages. It's an auspicious time. It's also the month of the harvest festival, Pongal, which is celebrated with great fervour throughout the state. Kolams, pujas, mass cooking, new clothes, decorated cows, an inexplicable exodus to the beach (on all manner of transportation), are part of the festivities, but there's also *Bhoghi,* which involves taking out all the old, rubbishy things from our houses and burning them on the sides of the streets. A paradoxical event that symbolizes the cleansing out, purging, or uncluttering of our lives, but in actuality, de-cleanses, poisons, and clutters up the air with all kinds of toxic fumes.

Nevertheless, this is where we return to our frayed shirts and threadbare sheets. To the Madras syndrome. To David Ogilvy's brilliant advertising gimmick – the shirt that's guaranteed to fade, the Madras checks, the untapped magic. As a city, it has the same special qualities of the simple checked shirt lying in your cupboard. It's what you reach for when you have nothing else to wear; it's what you return to over and over for its blissful familiarity. It's comfortable, doesn't overpower, isn't glossy, allows you to retreat or stand in the light. It's real. And as we approach this time of bringing out all the achievements of the year to see if they sparkle, it's easy to hold a sense of disgruntled disillusion. To complain that this shirt has had either too much or too little washing, water, or wear. It's easy to turn into a group of snivelling, self-pitying sods, the only ones in the whole country forced to mope about in front of our non-set-top-box-enhanced televisions to watch news 24X7 or Tamil film songs.

But still, it breathes, allows you to *be*. Still, it has the capacity to welcome, to startle. These are new days ahead of us – not of sprawling houses and coy girls in *pattu pavades* and ribboned double plaits. These are days of burgeoning Bollywood stars, coffee pubs, and call centres. Great romances can still be born here.

A politics of retribution

MUKUND PADMANABHAN

AN Ooty boarding school is the last place that would familiarize anyone with Tamil Nadu's politics. Although mine liked to regard itself as 'alternative', in many ways it was a typical sort of place. We learnt to eat brussel sprouts and rhubarb, rode mid-horses in the downs and spent our fortnightly 'Tuck' money on stickjaws and marzipan in the town bakery.

I doubt whether our motley bunch of staff members – which at different times included a kindly Irish matron, a sharp-tongued Australian art teacher, an urbane and immensely sophisticated Uttar Pradesh Muslim and a tweed-jacketed Principal with a passion for English – knew or cared much about the state's politics. If the English-speaking middle classes have a natural contempt for things political, then boarding schools such as mine only served to reinforce it.

In the latter half of the sixties, when I was still a young boy, I remember becoming aware that something important was brewing in Tamil Nadu through the hushed whispers of my teachers. In 1967, the Dravida Munnetra Kazhagam (DMK), led by the charismatic film scriptwriter C.N. Annadurai, overwhelmed the Congress and swept to power in the state. This change of guard was preceded by a fierce and emotional agitation against the imposition of Hindi – a protest that fired the imagination of students, led to self-immolations and rounds of police firing.

I do not recall our teachers speaking about the momentous happenings in the state in any detail. But it was pretty apparent that they regarded what was taking place as a bad thing. I guess we did too. Whether you cared about politics or not, back in those days the Congress was the natural party of English-speaking middle classes. That being so, anything opposed to it was viewed with an instinctive suspicion. I recall there was a lot of nudging and winking when the Swatantra Party's Piloo Mody visited our school. He was treated with the courtesy one would extend to any guest, but we were persuaded to believe he was unreliable, eccentric and entertained outrageous views about economic development. (Funnily enough, I recently heard someone refer to him as the Manmohan Singh of the sixties, a man whose ideas were before his time.)

Unlike the jocular Mody, the DMK didn't seem funny. Parties with strong regional identities based on language, caste and community are commonplace now. Back in those days, they seemed to pose a challenge to the country's very unity and identity. The fact that the DMK had advocated secessionism and formally renounced this plank in 1963 didn't help much either. For a certain kind of cosmopolitan Indian – or for the deracinated English-speaking upper classes as some would prefer to say – the emergence of forces such as the DMK felt like a real threat.

The margin of the DMK victory in 1967 was stunning, but few people could have foreseen that this election would mark the beginning of such a rapid decline of the Congress party. Neither could many have anticipated that Tamil Nadu – if you ignore the brief spells of President's Rule – would be under the rule of one of two major Dravidian parties for a period of almost four decades or ever since.

As you might expect of such a long period, this has been a time of both achievement and failure. The DMK opposed the Emergency and has consistently struggled for a more thoroughgoing and genuine federalism. Tamil Nadu is the country's sixth most populous state but one of the better-off in terms of both per capita income and growth. Advances in literacy rates and curbs in population growth have been achieved partly though innovative measures such as former Chief Minister M.G. Ramachandran's midday meal scheme. It was rubbished as a populist measure when it was launched in the early eighties, but the growing recognition of its social impact led the Supreme Court to direct all states to implement an MGR-style midday meal scheme in 2001, which it described as 'a joy – a living example of what can be achieved when quality safeguards are in place.'

On the debit side are such things as the substantial growth in corruption, a marked tendency towards intolerance and authoritarianism and a climate marred by a worrying, all-consuming and potentially calamitous political hatred. I will return to the last issue later, but a detailed balance sheet of credits and debits would be out of place in a rambling and personalized political essay of this nature. A more appropriate, even if somewhat flippant way of looking at Dravidian politics – the result of a movement born from ideology and protest – is to see how it fared in dealing with its enemies, with what it fiercely opposed.

Some commentators have portrayed the Dravidian political movement as having emerged out of the opposition to four principal evils – Brahminism, Hindi, Religion and Casteism. If this were so, then the four fell into two distinct categories. The first two enemies were pushovers; the last two have proved formidable, much too resilient to vanquish.

At less than 3% of the Tamil Nadu population, Brahmins were a cinch. Even though they continue to flourish in the private sector and the arts, their overwhelming dominance in politics and in government was quickly broken. In fact, the available evidence shows that the challenge to Brahmin domination had begun at the turn of the 20th century with increasing numbers of non-Brahmin castes being admitted to school and college. It was against such a background that the richer sections of the non-Brahmin castes founded the Justice Party in 1916, the ideological precursor to Periyar's Dravida Kazhagam and Annadurai's Dravida Munnetra Kazhagam.

Organizations such as the DK and the DMK were fighting Brahminism and not Brahmins. But waging a political campaign against the idea is difficult to sustain when its proponents have been rendered politically irrelevant and when they are not big oppressive landowners in rural areas. Dravidian parties prefer to ignore this, but on the ground, the real caste tensions exist between the non-Brahmin castes, principally between Dalits and other backward castes. Clashes between Thevars and Dalits reached a feverish pitch in the southern districts as recently as 1997-98. According to the state government estimates, at least 251 people were killed in caste violence between August 1995 and October 1998. Tense situations because of strained relations between the Dalits and the Vanniyars are not uncommon in Tamil Nadu's northern districts.

As for Hindi, the battle against its imposition was won at considerable human cost. But the fierce agitation forced the Centre to capitulate completely on the plan to make Hindi the sole official language. Non Hindi-speaking states were assured that Hindi would not be imposed as the sole language of communication between Centre and state governments as long as even one state objected. Moreover, the Centre made it clear that examinations for the central government services could be taken in any of the scheduled languages.

The battle against Hindi-imposition was won in 1965, months after the protests were launched. Today, the problem, as some Dravidian parties see it, comes from another and unexpected quarter: English. In a state where the political class, a fair section of it anyway, is obsessed about protecting the purity of the mother tongue, spoken or colloquial Tamil borrows heavily from English. Tamglish has been around decades before the term Hinglish was invented and, with every passing month, more and more English words seem to find their way into spoken Tamil.

Tamils recognize that English is a passport to social and economic betterment as much as anyone else in India. English medium primary schools have mushroomed in the state. Worried about this, the DMK government issued an order four years ago that Tamil be the sole medium of instruction in the state. However, the Madras High Court struck down the order; one of the arguments in favour of annulling it was that parents have a right about the choice of education they would like their children to be exposed to.

What about religion and casteism? Rationalism was one of the cornerstones of Periyar's historic and revolutionary self-respect movement, but Dravidian parties have made their peace with religion. In theory, the DMK still professes rationalism, but in practice it prefers to avoid addressing the issue. As for the AIADMK, it has given up even this pretence. During both her terms as chief minister, Jayalalithaa has made no secret of her religiosity and has gone out of the way to undertake schemes for temple renovation and for the welfare of priests.

As for casteism, what impact has the Dravidian movement – which culminated in four decades of Dravidian rule – had on the phenomenon? Periyar decried casteism and promoted intercaste marriages and reservations have been extended to benefit a slew of backward castes. But is caste sentiment less prevalent than elsewhere, for example, the neighbouring southern states? It is probably impossible to make such sweeping comparisons with any accuracy, but caste calculations have become an abiding feature of the polity. The 2001 assembly election saw a proliferation of outfits based either on caste or communal lines. Most of them were accommodated in the DMK-led front, which was possibly banking that the incremental votes they would deliver would count in what was essentially a bipolar contest.

The nascent Makkal Tamil Desam, founded by a former AIADMK minister, was accommodated with an eye on the Yadava votes in the southern districts. The Kongu Nadu Makkal Katchi was unabashed in its portrayal as a part of the Gounders and the Tamil

Nadu Mutharaiyar Sangam, as the name suggests, was a party for the Mutharaiyars. Added to these were other formations such as the Tamil Nadu Muslim United Jammait, a breakaway group from the Tamil Maanila Congress led by the late G.K. Moopanar, and the Thondar Congress, founded by a former state Congress president with an eye on gathering Nadar votes. As it turned out, these parties performed very poorly, leading some commentators to conclude that they were rejected by an electorate that found these upstart caste and communal parties simply unacceptable. But their poor performance must also be viewed in the context of the overwhelming defeat of the DMK-led front, which was all but trounced by the one put together by Jayalalithaa's AIADMK.

My first brushes with Tamil Nadu's politics came when I worked in what was then Calcutta for a now defunct weekly magazine. Among the occasional reporting assignments I did in what was then Madras was a cover story on who was then Jayalalitha. (She had not added the additional 'a' to her name at the time). This was in 1991 and Jayalalithaa had stormed to power with an enormous majority. She was still in her honeymoon period and the national press seemed fascinated with the new chief minister. Her tough and no-nonsense ways – which, among other things, was reflected in the manner in which she dealt with the LTTE – won her many admirers.

She had agreed to an interview. However, when the appointed day arrived, I received a call saying she was down with a sore throat and fever. Could the questions be faxed? She promised to answer them. The headline on the magazine cover we had designed read 'The Iron Butterfly' and I asked her what she felt about the description. I was struck by the force and intelligence of her reply. She pointed out that Iron Butterfly was used to describe Imelda Marcos, implying that she had nothing in common with the controversial Philippines leader. 'I agree with iron,' she said, 'but not butterfly.'

I returned to Kolkata and wrote an extremely flattering piece accompanying the interview, the kind of article that any politician would have been delighted with. Or so I thought. After the article was published, I spoke to the official who coordinated the interview. I was surprised to learn that he had been asked to convey to me 'Madams' displeasure with a line here and another there in the article. I cannot recall exactly what all her objections were. But apparently, she felt I was somewhat uncharitable about her role as a parliamentarian. There was also a suggestion that I had been too kind to her DMK rivals at one point in the article.

In some ways, this was my first lesson in Tamil Nadu politics. Criticism, even of the mildest kind, is frowned upon; a kind word about a political rival is regarded with disapproval. One year later, in 1992, I moved to Madras to work for the *Indian Express*. It was only then that I realized the extent of the bitterness and acrimony between the two major Dravidian parties, the DMK and the AIADMK. To the four evils they are supposedly waging a war against, either party could add the other as a fifth.

Political hatred is commonplace in India, but I suggest that what exists in Tamil Nadu has no parallel. The relationship, if this is the right word for it, between the DMK and the AIADMK is characterized by a total and all-consuming revulsion. So much so, politics is not a competitive game for power but a platform for pursuing hostile agendas. The consequences of such an attitude have already been extremely undesirable. How dangerous this can be in the long run is something that is not adequately recognized.

One way of examining the mutual hatred between the two big Tamil Nadu parties is by looking at the non-relationship between its leaders, the AIADMK's Jayalalithaa and the DMK's M. Karunanidhi – something that sets the tone for the non-relationship between those in the middle and lower rungs of their respective parties. To my mind, one somewhat trivial incident illustrates this non-relationship best. In February 2001, Jayalalithaa and Karunanidhi boarded the same flight from Madurai to Chennai, after completing a leg of campaigning for the Lok Sabha election. The very fact that they sat on opposite sides of the aisle on the same flight sent the press into a frenzy. Airline sources were questioned to find out whether they spoke to each other.

(No, they did not.) Did they at least exchange a hello? (Nope.) One newspaper described the fact that they were on the same commercial airliner as 'incredible'.

The vicarious interest provoked by an accidental encounter in an aircraft illustrates the extent of how personal (or impersonal) Tamil Nadu's politics has become. Even a hello between the two leaders becomes news. What originally caused the relationship to plummet to such an extraordinary low is not clear. But the one between Karunanidhi and the AIADMK's founder, M.G. Ramachandran (who split the DMK) wasn't quite like this at all. Underneath the bitterness lay a grudging acknowledgement, even respect, for each other. It is exactly this complex attitude that filmmaker Mani Ratnam attempted to explore in his emotional, and somewhat cloying, *Iruvar*. DMK flags flew at half-mast when MGR died in 1987 and Karunanidhi's generous condolence message suggested that their personal relationship outweighed their political differences.

In the early years, there were a number of incidents which sharpened the antagonism, the principal one perhaps being the violent incidents in the state assembly during Karunanidhi's short tenure as chief minister in 1989. Jayalalithaa alleged her 'dignity' and 'modesty' were assaulted by DMK MLAs, something they completely denied – resulting in two totally disparate accounts of the events. But if there was a time when the equation between the DMK and the AIADMK reached the point of no return, it was in 1996.

In that year, the DMK swept to power on a tidal wave of resentment against Jayalalithaa, who had completed her first term as chief minister. In alliance with G.K. Moopanar's newly formed Tamil Maanila Congress, the DMK made the 'corruption of the Jayalalithaa regime' its central campaign plank – a strategy that worked. So deep was the resentment against her rule that Jayalalithaa was defeated in her constituency (Barugur) and her party was virtually wiped out of the state's electoral map.

Having promised to 'expose Jayalalithaa's corruption', the DMK government was expected to conduct a few investigations against members in the previous regime. Nobody, however, could have anticipated the extraordinary scale of the exercise. Apart from Ms. Jayalalithaa, corruption investigations were launched against virtually every minister in her cabinet. A number of them were arrested (Jayalalithaa spent 27 days in remand) as were a few senior bureaucrats. At one time there were preliminary inquiries into approximately one-third of the total strength of IAS officers in the state. Of course, only a few of them reached the charge sheet stage.

As someone who spent a lot of time in those days meeting bureaucrats in the Secretariat at Fort St. George, I could not help being struck by how totally engrossed the state government was in this exercise. Key officials of the Karunanidhi regime spent more time on these cases than on their routine work. Clearly, there was and is no parallel – no comparable instance of a government initiating such a systematic and wide-ranging exercise to prosecute members of the political opposition. Some have argued that this was necessary because of the unprecedented corruption during the Jayalalithaa regime. Others believe that the huge landslide in favour of the DMK had led Karunanidhi to misread the situation. In other words, the corruption cases were mechanisms to place a judicial seal on Jayalalithaa's already finished political career.

As things turned out, Jayalalithaa performed extremely well in the Lok Sabha election two years later, a poll that saw a BJP-led government in place at the Centre. Having gained a critical toehold at the Centre, she began pressuring it to take action against the DMK government in Tamil Nadu. Her decision to pull the plug on Vajpayee in 1999 was a result of her frustration over the BJP's reluctance to do as she wanted – principally, its refusal to impose President's Rule in Tamil Nadu. Even before she returned to power in 2001, in an assembly election in which the DMK was all but routed, she had made one thing clear. She would do unto 'them' what was done unto her. There has been a worrying familiarity to the subsequent events. Karunanidhi and other DMK leaders were arrested, corruption cases slapped on a number of former DMK ministers and so on.

Such goings on in Tamil Nadu suggest that in their mutual hatred, the two principal players have forgotten that politics – even at its worst – is but a competitive game for power. It is not – or at any rate should not be – a mechanism for carrying out vendettas, for taking decisions that are vindictive or vengeful. The damage this has done to the state is not adequately recognized and the potential it has to harm it even further is rarely addressed. What is obvious in the meantime is that it is not merely the two parties alone that have been hurt by this acrimonious relationship. It is the state itself.

It has led to a situation where the bureaucracy is demoralized and, perhaps worse, is divided down the middle on the basis of political loyalties – either real of perceived. Even the judiciary and the press have not been free from the influence of such acrimony, which has resulted in a political attitude that suggests 'you are either with us or against us.' It has created a situation where the two parties are unable to make common cause even on issues that are vital for the well-being of the state – for example, the Cauvery water dispute. And it has consumed too much governmental time on such things as charge sheets and arrests, time much better spent on the larger issues of administering the state. In short, the implications of the politics of retribution in Tamil Nadu do not stop with the polity alone. They have a bearing on the very social and economic well-being of the state.

Weird, warped, or plain wonderful?

SCHARADA BAIL

IT was apparent quite soon after my arrival as a young bride 20 years ago, that Chennai, or Madras as it was then known, was very different from any of the places I had lived in before. It wasn't just the North-South difference, though this was the source of a big handicap in the beginning – my lack of Tamil. It was also in the very manner of absolute strangers. Somehow, in the first conversation, such people seemed to want to get to the roots of my identity. Was I a vegetarian or non-vegetarian? Did I live in my 'own' house or a rented one? Was I a Brahmin or non-Brahmin?

Having just arrived from Mumbai, or Bombay as it was then known, I found such a concern with matters personal amusing, irritating, disturbing or distressing as my mood and circumstances dictated. While I understood it as a need to slot me into neat mental categories, obviously important for people here, I could not help comparing it with the carefree cosmopolitanism of my Bombay upbringing. What did it matter if one's friends were Hindu, Parsi, Muslim or Christian? Why should the state of anyone's home concern us, whether it was in a *chawl*, a block of flats on Warden Road, or more discreet lodgings in Grant Road? We lounged at Regal or the Gateway, Kala Ghoda or Metro and never saw the insides of our friend's houses, far less probed into their eating habits.

So Chennai felt like moving back in time – a place where social, religious and cultural categories really counted for a lot. I was standing at a bus stop when a woman turned around and said to me, absolutely out of the blue, 'You are not from Madras, isn't it?' I confessed to the crime, out of sheer surprise. She nodded, comforted by her diagnosis being confirmed. 'I can make out by your jewellery,' she said. Her reference was to the silver I wore, in personal preference to gold which is the standard ornamental uniform for a woman from the South. Now, 20 years later, neighbours and friends view my continued preference for silver indulgently. Then, it was another factor setting me apart.

I railed and ranted at the provincial mindset as I perceived it, and burst into occasional tears (a pardonable excess of youth), till slowly, other aspects of Chennai's difference from other cities, especially the metros, began to sink in. The modest ordinariness of high achievers was something that seemed to characterize life around me. The elderly gentleman, quietly letting himself out of the gate to his house at 4.30 am in the morning, could have been a scientist at one of the country's leading research establishments (and often was). But that did not prevent him from going to fetch his own milk from the booth. Or the most celebrated nightingale from the South who would answer her own phone and artlessly respond to all callers without a trace of snobbery. I observed that humility and high personal and professional standards had a big place in Chennai's mind and heart, and this took away some of my initial discomfort. Over the years, this discomfort has changed to a fierce love for Chennai, the oddest of metros.

Unlike Mumbai, where Parsis provide sufficient lore in the chronicling of eccentrics and eccentricities, Chennai does not have a resident community of oddballs. But this in no way diminishes the possibilities of eccentricity creeping into many visible areas. In fact, Chennai is highly tolerant of many examples of 'way, way out' behaviour, which goes completely against its staid and stolid image of a conservative metro. Consider, for instance, our politicians. It was Chennai that first showed how dark glasses, usually synonymous with Mafia men, could actually be such effective instruments in the creation of a political persona. MGR's dark glasses are still the most distinguishing feature when rustic children dress up like him for fancy dress events. As for Mr. Karunanidhi's, they enable him to have a rosy-tinted view of the world, when everything else is quite literally, dark.

Other quirky accoutrements of Chennai's politicians have been the saree-matching capes that Ms. Jayalalithaa sported the last time she was CM, and the same-sex companion that she flaunts with impunity whether she is CM or not. In fact, this single appendage is the source of much grievance and resentment, but however much people may speculate about the exact nature of the companion's relationship with the CM, there is no denying that there is public acceptance of this arrangement.

There are other, darker aspects to the eccentricity of politicians that are only whispered about, but which border on the bizarre. These range from the tales of Karunanidhi marrying a Brahmin virgin when in his seventies to revive his political career (this has to be seen in the light of the Dravidian parties avowed anti-Brahminism, apart from being condemned from a feminist perspective!), to the many *yagnas* and *homas* performed by Jayalalithaa for the annihilation of her political foes (most people consider these to have had a supremely successful effect). In swallowing the superstitious, recidivist and reactionary eccentricities of its leaders, Chennaiites show a tolerance that is in keeping with the most avant-garde of the millennium.

In fact, when these eccentricities are brought into the public glare, through the medium of cinema, for instance, they are not well received. Thus, while Mani Rathnam's *Iruvar* was a film much loved by critics, it could not wow the box-office with its depiction of MGR's love life and Karunanidhi's, or its projection of Aishwarya Rai as the young Jayalalithaa. Perhaps this reluctance to focus publicly on the oddities of its leaders is also part of Chennai's very clear attachment to privacy for the famous.

For a city whose dwellers think nothing of probing into your personal life as soon as they meet you, Chennai is a city very committed to guarding the privacy of its celebrities. Nobody here, not even the models and film stars, much less the corporate big wigs or their wives, is rushing to make it to Page Three. In fact, the highest grossing film star of 2003, Vikram, lived in a modest rented house in Besant Nagar till he bought a larger place, and his wife works as a de-addiction counsellor at TTK hospital, unsought by any film journalists or society columnists. Their comfortable obscurity is in stark contrast to the media-savvy manoeuvering of Mumbai and Delhi, where the likes of Parmeshwar Godrej, Nina Pillai and Nafisa Ali pepper the newsprint with uncanny regularity.

The distinct social and cultural divisions in Chennai resonate with their own eccentricities. There is the genteel Brahmin, classical music and dance loving culture of the December music festival, and the robust, Dravidian, Chicken 65 and punch-up culture of the hoi polloi. When it comes to the music festival, it is difficult to know where eccentricities start and where they end. For instance, one can go and sit next to a gently dozing elderly lady 'rasika' at a music concert, who has her more alert, mufflered husband (any day when you do not actually sweat is extreme winter for Chennaiites, and calls for protection), sitting and moving his head in appreciation of the music, right beside her.

When Kadri Gopalnath's powerful saxophone strikes its opening notes, the lady gets up and notices. 'It's Kanyakumari,' she remarks to her husband, referring to Ms. A. Kanyakumari, who generally accompanies Kadri Gopalnath on the violin. 'She's wearing a mango-coloured saree, isn't she? She always does. Nothing but bright mango coloured silk.' Her husband merely grunts in acknowledgement of this bit of superior knowledge, but as an overhearing listener, your mind can be teeming with a hundred questions and observations.

Is it common knowledge that Kanyakumari only wears shades of sunflower yellow or bright mango colour? Does everyone know that she also gets up at 3.30 am every morning and has already bathed thrice and done many pujas before most people get up? What about this lady rasika and many like her and her husband? How do they manage to sleep in such damned uncomfortable chairs? Is the Chennai December festival a celebration of music and dance or a fiendish conspiracy to inflict torture hatched by cunning aliens? Weird thoughts come naturally in one's mind in these surroundings.

Ms. Kanyakumari is also not the only eccentric musician on public view in December. Kunnakudi Vaidyanathan, another famous violinist, has made his smeared-with-red-*sindoor*-forehead, accompanied by kindly leer, a familiar sight for many decades, apart from his special individual style of playing which consists of giving the violin strings regular 'pings' with his fingers in the midst of the normal bow plying. Balamuralikrishna can compete with Kunnakudi in appreciation of pretty young female 'rasikas', and his hair is growing a more jet shade of black in direct proportion to the passing years. Musicians are pardoned their highly individual styles and manner in Chennai, as are certain high-profile 'rasikas' like Mrs. Y.G. Parthasarathy, redoubtable head of a group of educational institutions, who arrives for concerts assisted by a three-footed cane, covered with chains of different stones and metals, and always sits in the first row, because that is where she belongs.

Cricket, like music, has its own passionate following in Chennai, and some very distinguished names of the sport have their special quirks. S. Venkatraghavan, current international umpire, former Indian spinner and captain, who was rumoured to have been a suitor to Hema Malini at one time, is also known for the choicest Tamil expletives that flow smoothly off his tongue. In fact, cricketers from the league level of the game swap his most memorable 'gems' among themselves. Another memorable character is T.E. Srinivasan, a right-handed batsman who scored oodles of runs against fast bowlers in domestic cricket. His talent and run getting were not sufficient to draw the selector's attention, however, and he made a late entry into the national team in 1980-81. When the Indians went Down Under to play the Aussies, T.E. is reputed to have declared, 'Tell Lillee T.E. is here!' in reference to the dreaded fast bowler of those days, a statement so brimming with confidence that it is a pity it was never put to the test as T.E.'s services were not called upon by the team management.

Customs and rituals may seem to be a sign of collective weirdness for some, but in Chennai they acquire a significantly dynamic form. The Kanchi Matha of the Sankaracharya and his junior Sankaracharya, exercise a powerful influence over Chennai society, just as globalization and western concepts do. What the Chennaiite, ever adaptable, does is to achieve a balance in habit and belief, to suit both. Thus, in the last couple of decades, New Year's Eve was an occasion for many Chennai citizens to head for their neighbourhood temple. What better way to usher in a bright new year than in the presence of God?

So, on New Year's Eve, the neighbourhood temple was jam packed by 11.30 pm, never mind if drunken revelers were shouting and screaming immediately outside. The nadaswaram and thavil were played to herald the New Year *darshan*, while the deity was hidden from view by a velvet curtain. Only when the temple clock showed 12:00 did this veil lift, to the accompaniment of audible gasps from assembled devotees. In addition, there was usually a scuffle, and much jostling and shoving to be the first to receive the *aarti* from the lamp that the priest had waved around the deity. In this adaptation of Western Gregorian calendar to Eastern worship everyone was happy.

Not so the Sankaracharya. This year, he declared in advance that the *Shastras* did not recommend this practice, as it clashed with the hour when the deity was at rest in the temple sanctum sanctorum. In conceding to the popular thirst for midnight darshan, he did not prohibit temples from staying open at the midnight hour, only advised that the 'aarti' flame be shown to devotees from within the sanctum, rather than be brought outside in the normal way. This was duly followed, so that from New Year's Eve 2004, temple-goers received their 'darshan' and were even spared their scuffle! If only this clever example of Hindu adaptability would teach something to Shiv Sainiks and VHP venomists.

Another year, the Sankaracharya had declared that it was auspicious for married women to receive green sarees from their parental homes. More green was sold that year than in any other time, and store-owners must have rejoiced at this particular harvest. However, the choice of the colour green for this pronouncement is not without its significance. Was the Kanchi religious head also asking his followers to take a more affectionate view of the adherents of another religion, for whom green is worthy of reverence? A definite shot in the arm for secularists.

In fact, for all its overt Hindu religiosity, Chennai finds it easier to keep the communal peace than some other cities because anti-Muslim sentiment is not rabidly expressed in the public arena. This is partly due to historical reasons – Muslim looters from foreign lands only managed minimal damage to the splendid Hindu temples and monuments in Tamil Nadu. It is also because of the cheek by jowl coexistence of orthodox Hindus, mostly Iyengars, but sometimes Iyers also, with Muslims. Triplicane in Chennai is a fine example of this, where, if you are a newcomer, and cannot find your way to the Sri Parthasarathy temple through the maze of lanes, some kind person in a skullcap and beard will give you directions. While leaders of the hate-spewing kind undoubtedly exist in Chennai's midst, so far, they seem to have been kept at bay by the necessities of Dravidian politics. Touch wood, and amen.

After two decades in this seaside metro, I am more at home with the quirky traits that make Chennai special, than I was as a Mumbai exile with youthful expectations. It is true that these 20 years have made Chennai more and more like the other cities in many ways – the same shops, malls, designer labels, restaurants that the other cities offer. But in many significant ways, Chennai retains its original spirit, its own special way of doing things, which is usually remarkably efficient and impressive.

Chennai does spoil you for other places, because the people who serve do it with an added personal touch, which makes the gesture far more than a casual thing. The times when I have had a vehicle breakdown because of a burst tyre, or engine failure in pouring rain, we have always been rescued by passers by, who, after picking you up to give you a lift in their car, discover that you live in the same street as their brother-in-law, or have a child in the same school as their niece. Many years of this has given me a different perspective on the personal questions too. So what if people are more than necessarily curious? They are also very often genuinely concerned about you as a person.

Besides, the lack of a need to maintain surface appearances is very reassuring in Chennai. As a friend of mine put it years ago, 'Bangalore's great for a visit, but I could never live there – people put on lipstick and chiffon in the morning when they go to buy bread and milk! Our Madras is the best, at least we can buy vegetables at our gate in a nightie, with our hair in an oily knot, and its perfectly ok!' For a city to retain this outlook in times of FTV is indeed remarkable.

In the final analysis, what Chennai has is plenty of individuality, rather than just eccentricity. While originality does lend interest to dull routine, and many Chennai practices might appear weird to denizens of other metros, Chennaiites themselves will cling to these examples of weirdness as an inseparable ingredient of the quality of life they perceive for themselves. Chennai is a city of very hard-working people, beset by water problems, ruled by strange leaders, and crammed with the latest gleaming cars in India. The fact that so many of its people seem to be marching to the beat of their own special drums makes it even more desirable.

Chennai: Madras

DEBORAH THIAGARAJAN

I NEVER acknowledged the name Chennai as an English name for Madras. It was always the name I read in Tamil script on the buses of the city. Chennai in Tamil script, Madras in English and spoken Tamil. Madras was a city that happily harboured this duality of language and name and was comfortable with both languages, at least among its college educated citizens. Language has been a source of pride among Madrasis, and it was common even in the '70s to hear Tamil speaking Madrasis converse among themselves in English, with mastery over both languages. As a young American woman arriving in Madras in 1970 with my Tamil husband, I took refuge and comfort in the prevalence of English while struggling to learn Tamil.

Language – this is an issue which has stirred Madras and its politicians over the last 34 years that I have been experiencing the happenings of Chennai. It is one of the keys to the character of the citizens of Chennai. The fixation with Tamil and English both hides and reveals many facets of what makes Madras such a charming and culturally significant city to live in. Madrasis regard the Tamil language as the key to the essence of their culture. English is their window to the wider world; Hindi, an imposition of an alien, aggressive culture trying to dominate. However, the reality today is that the knowledge of 'good' Tamil is dwindling among the children of Madras' elite thanks to English medium schools and, slowly, ever so subtly, the knowledge of Hindi is increasing, mainly through the cinema and TV.

Madras has a reputation of being conservative. And it is. It is socially conservative, but that has been changing rapidly during the last 10 years. The first lesson I learned was that the character and strength of a Tamil matriarch was kept happily camouflaged by her outward demeanour and dress: the Kanchipuram silk saree, diamond nose studs and earrings, sleekly oiled hair in a bun decorated with jasmine, a gold chain and *tali* around her neck and vermillion *pottu* on her forehead. Accompanying this traditional dress was usually a demure, almost languorous and self-effacing demeanour. This was the outward face of the married Tamil woman in Madras, carefully nurtured through her youth by a protective mother and a hoard of aunts.

Underneath this exterior, however, was a keen, thinking mind, often a progressive one. Unfortunately, up through the '70s it could usually only emerge into action with some twist of events, as was witnessed by the unleashed energy of Madras women during independence or as a consequence to the tragedy of widowhood. The choice before the Madras woman in the '70s was social compliance to restrictive rules or face the consequences of social ostracism. Most gave in, but the few who broke away discovered that they could make it on their own and gain respect for it.

During my early years in Madras I met enough of these strong women, who today are in their late '60s, '70s and '80s, to realize that they were made of a metal that few American women could compete with. And they influenced and inspired me and gave me the direction I took in my life in Madras. They also inspired their daughters so that it is now my generation of women who are working, and who have brought up their daughters as equals to their sons, living and experiencing the wider world in a way they could not. These children, like other young adults throughout India, are pushing the limits of Madras' conservatism and bringing in rapid change.

And how is Madras changing? There is the obvious. A soaring population, cars which choke the roads, a surge in new businesses and new business opportunities, including IT, the entry of many new players from all over India, an increase in MNCs and the foreign population that accompanies that, an unsolved problem of garbage and debris, the influence of the media, cable TV and the cinema for which Madras is famous, the rise of modern consumer oriented stores and a sprouting of good restaurants of every kind. Madras now boasts of Korean, Japanese, Thai, Fusion, Middle Eastern, French, Continental and Chinese restaurants alongside a whole range of Indian restaurants of every type and from every region. The restaurants with foreign fare are filled with the young, many of whom work in the thriving IT sector. The Indian style restaurants have a large family clientele. This is a huge change from the '70s when good restaurants were almost non-existent and eating out was considered something that you did only if you couldn't eat at home.

Madras has also become the consumer capital of India. Another aspect of the Madrasis which has influenced the character and pace of the city is the Tamil disdain for public ostentation in spending. Madrasis have never been ones to easily part with their money. Theirs has always been a low-key lifestyle. No outward show of money was considered positive. So with the consumer boom Madrasis are weighing the way they spend their money and they want value. If a product is tested and succeeds in Madras, I am told that the chances of it succeeding throughout India are high.

I admire this aspect of Madras. It makes life comfortable. No keeping up with the neighbours, no Rs 75,000 designer sets. Wear what you like, but don't make it too flashy unless, of course, it's your diamonds, the one weakness of the Madrasi. Gold, diamonds, Kanchipuram sarees, weddings, *the shastiathapurti* or renewing of the marriage vows at age 60, and family functions – these were what Madrasis traditionally spent their money on. Now it's education abroad for the children, health, the family home or flat, and consumer items which make for more convenient living. House pride has also made its appearance, and those with money are now indulging themselves in home decorations, altering the ascetic living environments of the '70s. The Kanchipuram saree is seen less and less, but still holds sway at weddings. Otherwise the salwar kameez and all its modern avatars are in.

For me Madras was a journey of discovery, like the opening of a lotus with each petal revealing one of its secrets. These secrets were the cultural avenues which Madras offered: learning yoga with T.T. Desikachari for nine years; experiencing the dance of Kalakshetra, the music of the home *katcharis*; a youthful Cholamandal artist's village which then held folk performances and craft workshops as well as art exhibitions, exploring Tamil and the literature of the Sangam period, the bhakti movement, learning Sanskrit, uncovering the history of the Pallava and Chola kings through inscriptions and temples.

For each of these discoveries there were dedicated people in Madras, scholars and experts willing to take time to help me in my learning. Malcolm Adiseshiah and the Madras Institute of Development Studies guided me in sociological explorations into caste; C. Subramaniam offered his political strategy insights when I organized an INTACH campaign on clean water and the Cooum River; Dashrath Patel explored his beliefs on design as I contemplated beginning the DakshinaChitra project to promote the traditional arts of the South; Chandralekha, the dancer, threw questions at me again and again to make me think; K.V. Raman and R. Nagasamy helped me unravel the complex history of temple and cult development in the South. I experienced the *guru shishya* tradition, alive and generous and so empowering in its support and encouragement. And this is all part of what makes Madras so culturally alive.

Madras is not a city which comes to you. This perhaps goes along with its understatedness. For many it is a long adjustment just in getting everyday life into order. But if one looks beyond to what the city has to offer there are treasures galore, if one is open to them, and many warm, accepting Madrasis willing to help or to listen.

In the world of culture Madras is beginning to truly blossom. I used to marvel at the raging controversies Madras *rasika*s had about Carnatic musicians. Each had his/her own like or dislike of styles and musical interpretations. These controversies, I decided, keep music at the centre-stage in Madras, and have resulted in the December Madras musical festival as an annual happening. The earlier *rasikas* were Mylapore Brahmins, stereotyped, maligned, but widely admired. They can be applauded for their work and for planting the seeds that are ensuring the continuity and evolution of Carnatic music in Madras.

Today culture in Madras is expanding to include the visual arts and more experimental programmes in theatre and dance. Madras is finally seeing the beginnings of good architecture, after at least 60 years of mediocre to bad buildings. As employment opportunities open up to the young they are moving out into new areas and developing interests beyond the traditional domains of their parents. This augurs well for the development of Madras as a major cultural centre in India. The city, however, still lacks that vital spinal cord which holds all the art forms and people working in the arts together.

Sometimes young people express a sense of feeling that they are working in a vacuum, but this is changing rapidly. New people and institutions offer new arenas and programmes; Anita Ratnam, Prakriti Foundation, and other cultural organizations for the Other Festival, innovative performances, music, lectures and special seminars; Amethyst for its venue for programmes and *adas*, and even the press for their recent Metro pages which bring the buzz and interest to the public at large. Corporate Madras has come forward to support these activities without whose funding they could not exist.

Yes, Madras is changing, and rapidly. I sensed the beginning pulses of this change in the early '80s and have witnessed the consequences. The destruction of some of Madras' and the South's most interesting heritage sites, a rupture of Madras youth from their parents' and grandparents' earlier rural roots, the intoxication with things new. No longer are the youth making the mandatory journey in their holidays to their *ur* or ancestral village for weddings and functions. This tie that bound Madras to its cultural practices has ceased in the last ten years. And yet, Madras has not let me down. Its cultural moorings are deep and they are loosening, but have not been lost.

I have admired these cultural roots. It was easy for me as a young married woman from a different culture to respect them and to be motivated to delve into them and their meanings, since people held them with pride. If they presented the world as black and white without the shades of grey which tend to engulf us today, it was all right. They presented a tableau which one could question, and hunt for the answers oneself.

Madras taught me that in the end it is what you believe, and what you feel is right for you, that you must do. I listened sporadically to the spiritual *swamijis* giving talks in Madras. They are ubiquitous, and they have lessons on life. Madrasis throng to them every season in great numbers, young and old, male and female. These lessons bring you back to the basics: they are about compassion, giving, peace of mind, the shrinking of the ego and the lessons of the Gita. I would like to think that Madras still harkens to the messages, even if in diluted form.

Madras still has a humanity about it that I have not noticed in a city like Delhi. There is no fear on the streets, no intangible feeling of aggression. Socialization on the streets or in shops reflects a harmony of interaction which stems from respect. Even eve teasing, the plague of young women in Indian cities, is largely under control in Madras although it has its moments. In a report on the position of women in India, Tamil Nadu, including Madras, took the number one place in the country for respect for women. When I first came to Madras I was shocked to see homes and settlements of the poor next to homes of the well to do. I now feel that this proximity had the effect of creating a balance in the minds of the people, by giving those less economically fortunate a personalized, and familiar face.

How long this peaceful integration of society will last is a question. The settlement patterns of Madras show a marked increase in slums and populations under the poverty line. Some of these slums are village communities which grew and were absorbed into urban Madras, and the environment. Though physically degraded, they are psychologically supportive of children and family ties. Others are not, but I cannot judge to what extent any of these families or settlements are able to access the opportunities of modernization. I am no longer in touch with these communities as I was when I worked on environment and malaria campaigns throughout the length and breadth of the city. I fear the anonymity that comes with high-rise, modern urban living of the western variety.

What has influenced me is the bright, attentive eyes filled with anticipation of the young children I have seen in the many city schools of Madras. It was into these school classrooms that I, with the untiring enthusiasm of V.R. Devika, brought in both classical and the folk performing art performances under the auspices of the Madras Craft Foundation from 1987 to1996. The MCF goal was to create an awareness of the rich diversity of the cultural forms of the South of India in the public and in the city schools. With INTACH's intervention for the preservation of the environment and the built heritage, I, as the INTACH Tamil Nadu convener for 14 years, initiated a larger environment and cultural preservation programme for the city.

But as cultural as Madras is, it has still to acknowledge the importance of its built and visual heritage, (even in 2004). Neither politicians nor bureaucrats have passed or supported heritage legislation to protect a single building, and protection, case by case, must still run through a court of law. The struggle to protect the built heritage, worldwide, must begin at the grassroots level with enough people clamouring for their right to their heritage and history over the demands of development for profit.

But in Madras only a handful of citizens were sufficiently concerned to be actively involved in fighting for this protection of the heritage. And so, the DakshinaChitra project I had conceived in 1984 of creating a museum for the promotion of the crafts, textiles and folk performing arts, grew into a larger conceptual project for the creation of awareness and promotion of the architecture and arts of the everyday lives of the diverse peoples of South India.

DakshinaChitra born as a concept in 1984, opened to the public in December 1996, and continues to evolve both in its programmes, exhibitions and institutional framework. It is a gift of Madras to Madras, the sustained work of all the people who volunteered their time and their effort, many in training me to be able to guide and sustain and persevere in the creation of DakshinaChitra, and many who joined the project out of their commitment to the significance of their culture.

Madras is inspiring. Dakshina-Chitra took root because Madras is a fertile Mecca for cultural projects. The public has also embraced the centre and we now have the wider Tamil middle class visiting, enjoying the reconnection to their rural roots, its architecture, folk performers and artisans. If DakshinaChitra continues to be a catalyst for new ways of looking at the past, at heritage and at its connection to the future, I will be rewarded. After all, only in Madras would the public, even the state government who gave the land, have encouraged and nudged a now, not so young American girl to embark on and accomplish a project she had barely envisioned 20 years back. A project which grew out of the way Madras and Tamil Nadu embraced her.

Virtual reality

GEETA DOCTOR

IT might seem a contradiction in terms, but the most successful artist working in Chennai, currently, is the dancer Chandralekha. She is not just the most dynamic face of contemporary dance in India, with her austere, yet erotically charged compositions of dance movements by a hand-picked group of dancers who perform with robotic precision under her silvery gaze, she epitomizes the absolute need to create a brand image, no matter what the art form, in today's competitive system.

'I have always had a keen sense of space' she explains. 'It's something that comes very naturally to me. It's spontaneous.' Her posters that are now collectors' items underline a strong design sense. Many of them, made to emphasize some aspect of female power, use traditional elements such as the eyes from a Durga mask, black, white, red or ochre colours and diagrammatic lines, or grids that frame the image in a boldly modernistic, meaning spare and bare, idiom.

As for those who enter her home, with its intimate, open-to-sky but stone wall enclosed theatre at Skills on the beach-front at Chennai, will acknowledge there is the same experience of a living space that has been informed by clear geometric lines. It is neither entirely new nor entirely traditional. The *mandala*-like enclosure of the theatre is approached by a meandering pathway through a garden that has become overgrown with trees that were planted over the years. For a performance, the viewer has to grope her or his way through a tangled semi-darkness, before getting a glimpse of the small opening that beckons with a tantalizing force of flickering light forms, merely glimpsed or hinted at on the stage deep inside a dark and apparently empty space. The audience sits on the ground within this space. The close proximity to the performance space, a bare platform with just a couple of pillars to frame it in vertical lines, not unlike the ones that Chandralekha has used in her posters, the use of dramatic lighting that bathes the area in a suggestion of gold or red against the blackness, underlines the effect of a painting that is in progress.

Since there could be no performance that would be complete without Chandralekha herself providing the *abhinaya* or emotional focus, even if only by her luminous presence on the side, one can only describe her as the central image of Devi, Durga, Shakti work-in-progress that is being created in dance on the stage. This again suggests that there is a link, a wholeness of inspiration that runs through her work – from her posters, her architecture, to her choreography – that however natural or instinctive is more in keeping with a traditional form of aesthetics, where every aspect from the visual to the aural to the performing arts, no less than the decorative and ornamental ones of textiles, jewellery, brass, gold or silver, were produced as alternative versions of celebrating the spirit within. Obviously, in most cases this was the image of the deity inside the main sanctum of the temple.

In today's world, where the artist is both a performer and the tangible or easy to digest object of the performative moment or skill, it is not difficult to accept that Chandralekha is herself the most visible aspect of her creative process. It is important that she remains successful for she is the icon of her success. Never mind that in her early productions, she felt impelled to criticise the old patriarchal forms of worship that extolled the virtues of this god or that within idolatrous modes of worship, of which dance was just the one that she appeared to be challenging.

Chandralekha has described the manner in which she choreographs her works elsewhere, so we shall not elaborate on this except to note that it is as she says a very 'instinctive' approach. She uses her dancers as moving signs on her canvas, drawing lines or patterns with their perfectly tuned bodies which are most often clad in her favourite colours – black-white-red-ochre, the earth colours, or blues and greens that are complementary.

Her use of esoteric names for the different compositions enhances the sense of being in touch with the mysterious and the eternal. There is none of the vulgarity associated with a title like 'Vagina Monologues' that one might encounter with a term such as *Yantra*, a composition in which she explores the female body, though they may both be exploring the same terrain as it were. Just as the visitor to her theatre has to traverse a wandering path, she too has found her inspiration in many of the till then little used traditions such as the *Kalari* or the Kerala form of martial arts, the Japanese Noh theatre, strong lighting techniques borrowed from western modern dance forms and placed them on the sturdy base of Bharata Natyam that has always been her starting point.

Far from forsaking tradition, she has transformed and made it an instrument that she can now use in her very own and distinctive manner. And patriarchy be damned, it is much more politically correct in today's context to focus on the female body that has found resonance both as a glamorous form and artistic fetish in a consumer driven society.

The reason that we have focused so extensively on Chandralekha's contribution to contemporary dance is because it underlines some of the problems that are faced by the artists working in the visual arts, painting and sculpture, in the South. By contrast, the Tamil Nadu artist today, working in a contemporary idiom is all but invisible.

'No one comes to our shows. Not the general public who say they cannot understand what we are doing, not the other artists who have already established a name for themselves, not the gallery owners who prefer to promote the work of outsiders and not the critics, who are controlled by the more successful commercial galleries.' This is the complaint made by any number of young artists who come rolling out of the Government College of Arts every year.

This time round it's been voiced by a group of four artists who graduated in 1998 and who have put together a group show that they have named 'Genesis'. Each one is talented in his own way. Alagar Raja works in fibreglass, wood and acrylic colours to create highly schematic compositions that have a 3-D effect to explore what he explains in Tamil are evocations to ideas of birth and rebirth and a search for matter before the actual moment of creation, what he calls 'The Birth of Art'. He has used traditional symbols of triangles and circles in a freewheeling manner that shows a serious engagement with his subject which is not trite or repetitive. Narayanan uses tight box-like frames to convey a highly textured and at times even richly layered effect, while Prabakaran has created a large tableaux installation in sand and painted strips against the wall.

Next to him, Ganesh uses shiny metallic objects – pieces of glass, discarded ball bearings, rows of staples and so forth – with equally reflective or brilliantly coloured metallic strips of paper, X-ray images and so on to construct a highly complex and convoluted impressions of a city seen from different perspectives. These young artists have used a great deal of skill and imagination to reinvent a landscape of ideas and feeling. Without an audience to look at their work, far less support it, it will be difficult for them to keep going. To add to their lack of visibility, the group is so idealistic about their art that they do not even sign their works as a mark of identification with the old tradition of master-craftsmen who worked in guilds. What can one make of such idealism except to shake one's head and tell them that they are making sure that no one will recognise them in today's highly individualistic culture.

'I've got resigned to the idea that no one will come to my shows,' says Natesh, an older artist, who is in fact highly successful as an installation artist with an appetite for huge outdoor constructions that are not meant to last longer than the time of the show, and who also works as an innovative stage designer. 'That's why I make my installations to last for just a couple of hours, and use materials that are easily available. I know that no one is going to buy my work and that I will die without getting any recognition. But that does not bother me one bit. I still wake up in the morning and feel full of energy. For instance, this morning, I applied a whole segment of my canvas with Cadmium yellow paint. It was wonderful, even though there was no one to see it.'

He laughs as he says this to the Genesis group. They merely look even more dejected. 'If only we can get one person to buy one of our paintings, we could afford to keep our show going for another week.' Their show is at the Lalit Kala Akademi gallery, that they all admit has the right kind of light and space for a work of their size and aspirations. But the truth is that without the support of a more dynamic commercial gallery person to promote their work, it will never attract an audience.

Soon enough, each one of the artists is bemoaning the fact that as long as they do not get the official patronage of those who occupy the places of power in New Delhi, it will be difficult for them to continue. Whereas in earlier times, it was possible for an artist from Chennai to seek his or her fortune in Mumbai at one of the better known galleries in the Fort area, not only are these now fully booked many months in advance, with each region aggressively branding and promoting their own stable of artistic productions, the 'Madras' artist, as anyone from the South is labelled, has little or no cachet at all. Even discerning editors, sitting in Mumbai, who commission work on the South Indian art scene groan in advance, 'No, please no more of those cheap decorative gimmicks you Southies love!' Or worse, 'We are so tired of the Cholamandal style,' as if every artist from Chennai, or the South could only come from Cholamandal. The South is just not 'sexy' enough, to use the current tabloid term to sell either articles or works of art.

How did this happen? As far as Tamil Nadu is concerned, the reasons are both historic and institutional. If we start with the pre-independence period and the years following that great moment of connectivity of thoughts and minds that took place in the country, we will find that the artists of that era were fired by a common impulse. This was both to free themselves from the restrictions of the colonial past and to rediscover and reinvent a manner of expression that would be simultaneously 'modern' and 'ancient' in keeping with the freshly articulated and officially sanctioned belief in a glorious past for the country. Artists were those who were entrusted with the task of unveiling these eternal truths that had merely been obscured through time and circumstance. South Indian artists felt particularly privileged. They could actually boast of a near unbroken tradition in many areas of artistic endeavour.

With the impetus given by a charismatic figure such as K.C.S. Paniker, who was not only Principal of the College of Arts, but who eventually went on to be a founder member of the Cholamandal Artists Village just outside Chennai, the best-known experiment in the South that would combine the living tradition of crafts with the infusion of artistic techniques and ideas brought in from all sides but particularly the West, there was a veritable explosion of talent that nurtured several gifted persons. One has only to mention persons like Redeppa Naidu, Sultan Ali, P.V. Janakiram and S. Dhanapal belonging to the first wave of artists who combined both streams, the old and the new, while retaining a strong stamp of their own selves in their work to demonstrate this.

A second wave of artists amongst whom we may name Viswanathan, S.G. Vasudev, S. Nandagopal, K.V. Haridasan, P. Gopinath, C. Douglas, who are still very active, and others like V. Arnawaz, Jayapal Panicker and K. Ramanujam, who are no more, established the idea that there could be a group of artists who might belong to the same place, but who worked in a highly innovative and individualistic manner.

Apart from those who had an affinity with Cholamandal, there were those who were more closely identified with the College of Arts. Among these are L. Munnuswamy, Santhana Raj who belong to the old guard and R.B. Bhaskaran, K.M. Adimoolam, Dakshinamoorthy of the next generation, with highly gifted individuals such as Thota Tharani, Rm. Palaniappan and Achuthan Kudallur belonging to neither faction but floating somewhere in between.

From the very moment that it was conceived, the Cholamandal Artists group managed to create an impression that they were somehow separate and enjoyed an exclusive right to represent Tamil Nadu's artistic heritage. Whether they were perceived as living in a citadel of artistic privilege meant to keep out outsiders, or as a closed community of self-serving artists, can be endlessly debated. It is certain, however, that they managed to evoke a long lasting hostility among the rest of the community of artists living in Chennai. Indeed, we might even say that it is because they were 'the community' of artists no other group has felt secure enough to survive as a group, or even want to be seen as a community of artists.

The real sufferer is, as we have seen, the fresh entrant into the artistic field. There is no one to act as a mentor or guide to the outside world. The decline of the artist's role as the keeper of the nationalist image or inner flame, also implying a lessening of importance at such venues as the once highly publicized and popular Triennales and Biennales that took place at the centre of privilege and position, New Delhi, the chance that artists from far-off places could be seen and have the opportunity to see for themselves how other artists were working, has also declined. This has increased the sense of isolation that the artist from Tamil Nadu now faces. Unlike his or her peers in a place like Kolkata that too suffers from the same political and institutional isolation, there has been no popular movement in the arts which has come to the rescue of the individual artist.

What did invigorate the public imagination was, of course, the Dravidian movement. Not only did this replace the old ideals of a pan-Indian consciousness, it introduced another very powerful medium

– cinema. Without going into further detail, it suffices to say that the cinema became as all-encompassing as religion was at one time. The actors who played the role of various gods and triumphal heroes and gently smiling Mother Goddesses and voluptuous heroines had little trouble in morphing into the real life saviours of the people. As is well-known, the models that were imitated drew on Soviet style realism to create images of invincible power, kindliness towards the poor, a lover of literature and so on.

The traditional artists who had once painted the murals in temples were effortlessly absorbed into painting the film sets and fantastical props that went into creating this parallel world. Their apprentices would start their careers painting the giant billboards, the street-level slogans, the crude wall pictures that began to proliferate on auto-rickshaws, lorries, push-carts, and on places of popular usage such as barber shops and fruit and *paan* stalls. Initially, these brightly painted banners or billboards promoted the film stars. At a later stage, the film stars and their creators, the endlessly quoted script-writers of witty dialogues and easily imitated lines of banter and repartee became the leaders of the Dravidian movement and its various offshoots and soon it was they who, in their dual garb as politicians-saviours of the masses, dominated the Chennai skyline.

With so much competition, the master painters of these billboards borrowed their techniques from many different sources. Their images owed as much to Ravi Varma and his favourite portraits of Indian womanhood in all her pan-Indian yet also Europeanised glory and the Impressionists as to more traditional Indian sources depicting the various *rasas* or moods laid down in the canons of dance and theatre. So it was that a film savvy crowd walking beneath these gigantic billboards could easily assess the gamut of emotions being presented to them by just registering the main colours – red for passion, purple and black for evil, golden yellow for goodness and, of course, pink for the hero and heroine – no matter what the Dravidians' truth to skin tones might be.

Not only did this coarsen the visual language, the type of reality that these painted vistas created in the public mind – of gardens filled with variegated flowers, with a small Japanese style wooden bridge across a pond filled with lotus blooms, a snow clad Mt. Fujiyama perhaps at the back or brilliant sunrises (many of them carrying not-so-hidden symbols denoting the party in power) – became the standard. These very same dream landscapes are now sold as laminated posters or mounted works of 'art' that are hung inside most homes to serve as indication of the person's individuality. If the Ravi Varma prints of the goddess of good fortune still dominate the more public areas of commerce and prosperity such as the entrance to a home or office, the framed pieces of chocolate box scenery showing nature's bounty fulfil their complementary role inside the private office, doctor's den, or living room. As though to underline their importance, most television serials recreate homes that have the same stereotypical landscapes on their walls.

Is it a surprise then that the Tamil Nadu artist finds himself in such splendid isolation? Despite such a monumental neglect, there is still much to rejoice however. There are many instances of individuals fighting back, indeed even rejoicing in their solitude. There are sculptors like S. Swaminathan who works using large blocks of granite that he chisels in rough chunks as though in homage to the great monuments of the past; or Raj Thiagarajan, an industrialist turned sculptor in his spare time, who fashions small pieces of plasticine into minimalist forms that are imbued with primitive strength after they have been chiselled and polished by a group of traditional stone sculptors; A. Balasubramanium who works in 3-dimensional compositions as large and lifesize as himself (since they are plaster casts that he's taken of himself) and which have already earned him wide acclaim; or S. Dinakar Sundar who works on the specially treated leaves of lotus flowers; Jacob Jeburaj and B.O. Sailesh from Cholamandal, who create installations and work at different locales and make use of a wide variety of materials; or P.G. Dinesh a young artist from Kerala, who lived at Cholamandal for some time, whose feline series and recent box-like compositions show a sense of defiance in the face of neglect.

They may appear timid at first. They may find it difficult to speak in perfect English sometimes, though they have mastered the art of communication having travelled to the outside world. They may not project the glory of their national or regional affiliation or make special claims for an identity that might give them a fleeting sense of belonging. They may not create an art movement. Nonetheless, they are filled with a determination to forge ahead creating their own reality out of their fractured heritage.

The music season

SRIRAM V.

THE music season has its origins steeped in history. From time immemorial, the month of *Margazhi* (December/January) has been considered particularly sacred, as Lord Krishna in the Bhagavad Gita states that among these months he exists as Dhanur masa, which is the Sanskrit equivalent.

Not surprisingly, it has been the practice among temples in Tamil Nadu to offer special worship to the deities during the month. No weddings are conducted during this period and no material transactions are undertaken by the orthodox as they believe that all of their waking moments are to be spent in the contemplation of the divine. Among the Vaishnavites this month is held in great reverence, for it was when Andal, the only lady *Azhwar* (12 divine saints), composed 30 verses on Lord Vishnu called the Tiruppavai. The Vaikunta Ekadasi falls around the middle of this month and the verses of Andal and other Azhwars are sung on all days. The Saivaites celebrate the Ardra Darshanam when the asterism Tiruvadarai is in the ascendant. On that day, Lord Nataraja is said to have danced for the pleasure of his devotees, Patanjali and Vyaghrapada.

Music and dance can thus be said to be have religious sanction during this month. However, it was only at the beginning of the 20th century that the season as we know it today became crystallised. With the decline of the Tanjore court from 1799 and the death of Tipu Sultan the same year, Madras emerged as the new centre of power. It attracted businessmen such as the Nattukottai Chettiyars and the Komutti and Beri Chettis who all settled in Black Town (now called George Town). The Mudaliars followed suit. Brahmins, both Telugu and Tamizh speaking from Tanjore and Tirunelveli moved in, attracted by better employment prospects. The establishment of the High Court in the 1860s, created a new breed; the lawyers, who were to dominate the city for over a hundred years. Landowners and royalty followed suit. All these people were patrons of music and soon Madras became known as the musical capital.

In 1927, the Congress party session was to be held in the city. Foremost amongst its organisers was S. Satyamurthy, the famed lawyer, theatre actor, orator and freedom fighter. Given his friendship with the musical fraternity, he pressed for the organising of an All India Music Conference to coincide with the party session. This was agreed and the conference and exhibition of musical instruments was held at the Spur Tank, Madras, beginning from 24 December 1927. Concerts were held at a *pandal* erected in the Spur Tank and conference deliberations were held at the Museum Theatre.

During the discussions it was proposed that an academy for music be set up in the city. Thus came about the Music Academy, which was incorporated on 22 January 1928, with U. Rama Rau (noted physician and Chairman of the Legislative Assembly, Madras) as President. The Academy was formally inaugurated on 18 August 1928 by Sir C.P. Ramaswamy Ayyar at the YMCA Buildings, Esplanade. The Academy began holding the occasional concert and it was during its first annual conference in 1929 that it was decided that a week long music festival be held to coincide with Christmas week. The logic was sound. The courts were closed during that period and the sahibs were having several rounds of merrymaking. The native society leaders were at a loose end and this gave them something to do.

The Music Academy, however, came to be dominated by the Tamizh Brahmin lobby and the Andhra element decided to set up the Indian Fine Arts Society in the mid-1930s. Both sabhas organised music programmes in December and both operated from the then cultural hub, North Madras or George Town. By then Mylapore was fast emerging as a choice residential area and music began gravitating to it. The Academy began a long journey south, holding its conferences sequentially at the Senate House (east Madras), Royapettah (south centre) and finally Mylapore (south) where it functioned for many years from the Rasika Ranjani Sabha premises and its surroundings before moving into its present building in 1962.

In 1941, the Justice Party, the prevailing anti-Brahmin sentiment and, above all, a rise in awareness of the beauties of the Tamizh language saw the birth of the Tamizh Isai Sangam. This was the third sabha of consequence and its decision to hold music programmes during Christmas week led to a raging debate in *The Kalki* and other papers as to the viability of three sabhas existing in the city. Then in 1945 came the Tyaga Brahma Gana Sabha (Vani Mahal) to cater to the residents of T. Nagar. By the early 1950s, came the Mylapore Fine Arts Club and the Sri Krishna Gana Sabha. It was, however, in the 1970s that the sabha boom actually happened, resulting in the situation as we know of it now with 70 odd sabhas organising over 2500 programmes spanning six weeks.

The music season usually kicks off by the last week of November, with a few small sabhas beginning their programmes earlier than others. Many of the city sabhas do not have premises of their own and consequently they need to plan their programmes in advance of the biggies in order to utilise available venues. For instance, the Kartik Fine Arts begins its programmes on December 1 at the spacious Narada Gana Sabha venue, where it continues till the 15th. That is when the Narada Gana Sabha begins its own programmes and so the Kartik Fine Arts moves to the RR Sabha premises. By the 21st, the RR Sabha begins its own programmes and so the Kartik Fine Arts moves to Anna Nagar where it hosts a series of Tamizh based music concerts at a college. The Kartik Fine Arts operates out of four different locations successively.

The big sabhas and many of the older established ones either have premises of their own or long standing rented venues and therefore do not suffer from this problem. Many of the fledgling sabhas simply operate out of the nearest *kalyana mantapam* (marriage hall), hotel or school premises. These are not built with acoustics in mind and hearing music in such places can be nothing short of torture.

The first week of December sees the influx of Indians from abroad. Earlier such visitors had to perforce stay with relatives and friends, with the New Woodlands Hotel being the only lodging nearby. Now there is a proliferation of hotels and paying guest accommodation, the latter offered by parents with children living abroad and whose flats are much larger than what they really require. The Woodlands continues to operate at full capacity nevertheless.

It is quite simple to spot the NRI among the crowd of local attendees. The NRI typically clutches a mineral water bottle, has a handycam (which he/she surreptitiously uses to record concerts till noticed), has a concert and song guide in hand and sports ethnic clothes (saree/dhoti) which do not wear well. They also have repetitive tales to tell of how they hosted a musician when he/she came to perform at Milwaukee or Chatanooga and based on this tenuous connection will try and meet up with the musician once again and re-establish contact. The poor musician, no doubt having accepted a three month overseas tour, will oblige, in anticipation of some much longed for *tayir sadam* in the US.

For the musicians the season begins looming large even by the middle of August when they are approached by sabhas and booked for concerts. Fans keep a tab on each artiste's popularity by counting the number of performances during the season. If an artiste suddenly drops down in the concert count from the previous year, the rumour mills begin to work overtime. Voice failure, miscarriage, divorce – all these are speculated on and analysed.

Overseas sabhas too keep a track of performances during the season and overseas tours are often decided on this basis. All this puts pressure on the artistes and many are forced to accept more concerts than their stamina permits. There are only a few who set a firm limit on the number of performances. But that requires great courage. Most artistes prefer to run the risk of cancelling concerts at the last minute rather than not accept them at all.

Next comes the awards fever. Sabhas begin announcing their awards by the middle of September. Carnatic music has never been free from awards, but it was only in 1942 that the Music Academy decided to award the President of its annual conference the title of Sangita Kalanidhi. The Indian Fine Arts Society followed suit with its Sangita Kala Shikhamani. Today we have over seventy awards given during the season by sabhas big and small. In terms of money, they mean little, but artistes consider them as appendages to personal prestige and accept them regardless. It is not a surprise to see an artiste receiving the Sangita Kalanidhi, also receive an obscure award with a cash component of Rs 1000 from a two-year-old sabha operating out of a kalyana mandapam.

By mid-December, the season is in full swing with the Music Academy and its close parallel the Narada Gana Sabha having begun their festivals. Artistes and audiences have a tough time keeping track of various concert dates and programmes. The smaller sabhas stick to evening concerts by prominent artistes. The bigger ones have full day programmes. Mornings are devoted to lecture demonstrations, afternoon concerts are free and showcase young talent, while evening concerts are ticketed and feature the big stars.

The vernacular and English newspapers and periodicals bring out special supplements on Carnatic music, with profiles of artistes past and present. Websites devoted to music provide schedules online which are used by the tech savvy. All sabhas bring out booklets comprising their own schedules, with the Academy's being a glossy affair (but of late full of factual mistakes and printers devils). Kannan's *Season Comprehensive Guide* is an integral part of the season. Brought out single-handedly in earlier years by a bank official, it now receives sponsorship, but the effort remains Kannan's own. It lists concerts by dates, venue and artistes. There are many reference books of songs that help lay audiences identify *ragas*, *talas* and composer names. The problem arises when songs in different ragas have the same opening lines and that is when the knowledgeable person (who is sitting in the next seat, with a faintly superior air) comes in useful.

Canteen facilities are a major attraction. Four sabhas have established themselves on the strength of their culinary and musical fare. These are the Music Academy, the Narada Gana Sabha, the Mylapore Fine Arts Club and the Sri Parthasarathy Swami Sabha. The last named, around 103 years old, was however a late entrant to the December season. In the old days, Krishnamurthy of the Music Academy canteen was a treasure whose Kashi halwa was relished by many. The chef supreme at the Music Academy now is 'Mountbatten' Mani. He acquired this prefix after being reportedly praised by the Viceroy himself during a lunch at the Raj Bhavan, Madras. Mount Mani paid Rs 1.30 lakh for bagging the contract at the Academy this season.

He is well patronised by music lovers and others who simply came to have a meal or snack. But Mount Mani pales in comparison to what three brothers have been upto in the other sabhas. Arusuvai Natarajan, the eldest, caters to the populace at the Sri Parthasarathy Swami Sabha and the banner that announces him as the chef is larger than the sabha's own. His brother Jayaraman holds sway at Narada Gana Sabha, while youngest brother Kannan operates from the Mylapore Fine Arts Club.

All three brothers have made the season a food festival in its own way. Natarajan specialises in full-scale meals while the others top the charts by way of snacks. It is a common sight to see artistes relaxing in these canteens after their performance, fawned upon by fans. Old timers remember with fondness such epicures as Maharajapuram Viswanatha Iyer, Dr. S. Ramanathan and M.D. Ramanathan coming to the canteen and discussing matters musical and otherwise with those present. Some of the more fastidious are of the view that canteens dilute the importance of music, but a sabha without a canteen is perceived to be dull fare.

Music fans are themselves divided into three groups. There is one which is never satisfied with what is offered now and claims that with Semmangudi no more all that was good in music has passed on. Yet this group continues attending concerts, always hoping of hearing something that will recreate old memories. This group is, however, best avoided. The second follows a single idol (whoever that may be) from sabha to sabha. They will not countenance listening to any other artiste. The third is the one that really keeps the season going. With eclectic tastes and preferences, a growing knowledge and curiosity they throng the sabhas.

How do the artistes, having to cater to as many as 21 concerts in the month, often to the same audience, manage to offer variety? A lot of planning is involved and several artistes learn new songs for the season in order to offer something new every time they sing. Yet the season does put them under a lot of pressure and it is only the most hardy and seasoned performers who are able to take December in their stride. In addition, the cool weather of Madras during the season causes a plethora of throat problems.

Waiting to catch the artiste at an unguarded moment and looking for an opportunity to pounce on them, are the critics who represent various dailies and periodicals. Each one has his or her own favourites whom they assiduously promote. The critics, often over burdened with too many concerts to attend, usually write the most perfunctory of accounts with little depth. Gone are the days of detailed analysis that Kalki or Aeolus (S.V. Seshadri) were capable of.

The electronic media with its mega serials offers tough competition to the season. 8.30 pm usually sees a thinning of audiences as they prefer to go home and watch the soaps. It is only the top two or three artistes and that too on a good day who are able to retain a full house till the end. Out of deference to changed times the concert duration has also been reduced from the earlier four hours to two and a half. A rather innovative series of programmes is the Margazhi Maha Utsav, the brainchild of a private production house. A series of concerts are held from 1st to 15th December at the Chettinad Vidyashram (among the best auditoriums in the city). These are open to all and generally attract record crowds. The concerts are recorded and telecast live over a private channel from the 15th to the 31st December. Sponsorships have poured in and this could be the way of the future.

The season as we know it, is not a commercial success. Most sabhas, barring the top ten, are operated by fly by night operators. Despite heavy gate collections, artistes are fobbed off with a mere pittance. The prestige that the season has acquired, however, forces artistes to accept these terms in order to be simply seen (and heard). Sabhas largely thrive on sponsors who view the whole event as a charity. The other commercial interests of the city such as hotels and shopping malls do not participate in the season, thereby preventing it from acquiring a broader appeal.

The government has remained indifferent, which according to many, is a positive thing. The city's infrastructure – transport, roads and accommodation – all come under severe pressure and this has only worsened over the years. The crying need is for buses to transport audiences to nodal points, but even this has not been thought off. Most sabhas were built during the days when there were few cars and these buildings have handkerchief size parking lots. The chaos in the surrounding areas during the programmes can only be imagined. The younger generation remains largely untouched and the season also has a Brahmin tag attached to it. Fortunately, music heritage walks, screening of vintage films and the music quiz have all somewhat increased the appeal of the season.

Yet it is that time of the year when Carnatic music makes a statement and manages to hold its own against television, cricket, cinema and other entertainment. Even if only once a year, it resurrects itself and stands out, testifying to the eternal nature of its appeal.

Two people, one industry

BARADWAJ RANGAN

TAMIL cinema has existed for over eight decades, and each of these decades has thrown up stalwarts in several fields. So it may appear strange to single out a film of the nineties made by a technocrat of the eighties – Mani Ratnam's *Iruvar* – as the work that defines Tamil cinema, as we've known it so far, as it is today, as it heads into the future.

Even if you agree that Ratnam is a sublime storyteller, a composer of poetry on celluloid, you could say he isn't the most original in terms of content. *Mouna Raagam* (A Silent Symphony), the film that put him on the map, was essentially a reworking of Mahendran's *Nenjathai Killaathey*, itself a silent symphony that emphasized mood over dialogue in telling the story of a woman (Suhasini, before she became Mrs. Mani Ratnam) who has to let go of a past love in order to come to terms with her present husband. With poems on celluloid that include *Mullum Malarum*, *Metti*, *Poottaadha Poottukkal* and, especially, *Udhiri Pookkal*, Mahendran proved himself a sublime storyteller almost a decade before Ratnam.

Even if you agree that Ratnam is a genius with form, you could say that he isn't the first who made stylish flourishes a hallmark of his ventures. There was, for instance, C.V. Sridhar in the sixties who, right from his directorial debut with *Kalyaana Parisu* – the box-office bullseye that combined the eternal love triangle with the timeless comedy of Thangavelu – made a name for himself as a purveyor of classy, sophisticated products. A *Then Nilavu* or a *Nenjil Or Aalayam* or a *Kaadhalikka Neramillai*, Sridhar films all, in those days was considered the work of a genius with form.

Even if you agree that Ratnam has a gift for mining drama out of controversial, never-before-seen subjects, you could say there have been others with similar penchant for going into uncharted territories. S. Balachandar, in the fifties, made the first Tamil movie without songs or dances – *Andha Naal*, a Roshomon-like examination of truth that dared to portray Sivaji Ganesan as an anti-hero, as a traitor who sold his country's secrets to the enemy.

Later, another similarly-named director, K. Balachander, broke rules and expectations – right from *Neer Kumizhi* (his debut, about the ephemeral nature of life) to *Arangettram* (about a Brahmin woman taking to prostitution to support her family), an *Aboorva Raagangal* (a love quadrangle involving two parents and their children) and *Thanneer Thanneer* (an indictment of the political scenario that couldn't even bring water to a parched village in Tamil Nadu) to *Vaaname Ellai* (about a group of youngsters who make a suicide pact).

Yes, for all of Ratnam's terrific talent with form and themes, he wasn't exactly a pioneer in these areas. More precisely, there were others before him who, for their time, accomplished many of the feats we associate with Ratnam today.

Yet, I pick him as *the* representative of Tamil cinema simply because of what befell him – a stroke of serendipity that placed him at the right place at the right time. He happened to be there when the quality of most mainstream movie-making in Tamil was abysmal, when the time was ripe for someone to step in and herald a change.

He happened to be around when fresh talents like cinematographer P.C. Sreeram – whose interest in the offbeat was evident in his participation in doomed ventures like *Meendum Oru Kaadhal Kadhai*, and who shot Ratnam's *Nayakan*, *Thirudaa Thirudaa* and *Alai Paayuthey*, among others – were available for like-minded filmmakers to collaborate with. Most importantly, he happened to be there when India was opening up in terms of awareness through increased and improved communications, when good films from India were beginning to be appreciated throughout the country and abroad.

Saying that Ratnam was simply at the right place at the right time isn't an effort to run down his genius; it's simply recognizing that had he come on to the stage even a few years before he actually did, he would have probably ended up like a Mahendran or a Balu Mahendra, treasured by the Tamils but unknown elsewhere. None of the avant-garde efforts before Ratnam's time – Rudraiah's *Aval Appadithaan*, for instance – managed much awareness. Nor did any of the filmmakers from other regions – Karnataka's Girish Kasaravalli or Kerala's Adoor Gopalakrishnan – ever manage Ratnam's level of popularity. In fact, it wouldn't be much of a stretch to say that were it not for Ratnam and his *Roja*, which spanned the proverbial Kashmir to Kanyakumari both in terms of its setting and its acceptance by audiences, we wouldn't even be talking about Tamil cinema on an all-India level today.

The masses of Tamil Nadu may not always line up for Ratnam's fare – it's always the action-cum-sentiment packed *masala* entertainers that make the big bucks – but his is the name synonymous with Tamil cinema outside of Tamil Nadu, outside of India, and his underrated, underperforming *Iruvar* is a mirror of the many things Tamil cinema has been about, is about, and probably will be about.

Iruvar is the story of aspiring actor Anandan (Mohanlal) and writer Tamizhselvan (Prakash Raj) who become friends and then fall apart. The aspiring actor, the writer and the key female character (played by Aishwarya Rai) are based, respectively, on M.G. Ramachandran (MGR), M. Karunanidhi and J. Jayalalithaa – so the film is, first and foremost, a marriage of cinema and politics, much like Tamil cinema, much like Tamil Nadu itself.

Tamil movies have always had strong ties to politics – the thirties *Thyagabhoomi* which wove real-life footage of Mahatma Gandhi into its story of a Brahmin priest espousing Gandhian ideals like the eradication of untouchability, the fifties *Parasakthi* that brimmed with Karunanidhi's fiery anti-Brahmin and pro-Dravidian rhetoric, *Yezhavathu Manidhan* (that used Bharatiyaar poetry to underscore its political themes) and *Kann Sivandhaal Mann Sivakkum*, even the routine masala fare today that frequently features politicians as corrupt villains. The state too began its affair with films when K.B. Sundarambal became the first star to be nominated to the Madras Legislative Council, and the government has, at different times, been headed by screenwriters (C.N. Annadurai, M. Karunanidhi) and actors (MGR, J. Jayalalithaa, V.N. Janaki).

Iruvar means duo – The Duo is what it was called in film festivals – and the story is dominated by two people, the MGR figure and the Karunanidhi figure. Tamil cinema itself has, for the longest time, embraced the concept of pairs. In the movie, Tamizhchelvan, with his interest in poetry, comes across as the more classy person, while Anandan's appeal is more directly to the masses, and this demarcation was shared by MGR in real life with Sivaji Ganesan, the other hero that constituted the duo that ruled Tamil filmdom for decades.

The latter, who began his career with *Parasakthi*, rose to become the sort of classy actor who could (and would) play anything from historical (*Veerapandiya Kattabomman*, *Kappalottiya Thamizhan*) mythological (*Thiruvilayaadal*, *Saraswathy Sabatham*) social melodramas (*Motor Sundaram Pillai*, *Uyarndha Manidhan*, *Vietnaam Veedu*) to just about everything else. MGR, on the other hand, went after the masses, carefully preserving his on-screen image of the good samaritan who defended those who couldn't defend themselves – the Robin Hood re-dos like *Malaikallan*, quasi-historicals like *Naadodi Mannan*, or later films tellingly named *Thozhilaali* (worker) and *Rickshawkaaran* (rickshaw-puller). After the MGR-Sivaji duo, of course, came the rule of another twosome, the classy Kamal Haasan and the massy Rajnikanth, whose roles often project an MGR-like saviour of society and whose MGR-like rumblings about politics have become increasingly loud.

Iruvar details a slice of Tamil Nadu politics that's clear only to a people who have been weaned on the MGR-Karunanidhi-Jayalalithaa interplay in real life, and hence harks back to a time when Tamil cinema was regional to the core. The film does not translate well across cultures, unlike director A. Bhimsingh's hugely successful 'Pa' series of family dramas – *Paavamannippu*, *Paalum Pazhamum*, *Padiththaal Mattum Podhuma*, *Paarthaal Pasi Theerum* – which were Tamilian in flavour but lent themselves to translation and interpretation into other languages and cultures.

Many of the early landmarks of Tamil cinema – *Poompuhar* (based on Silappadhikaaram, the ancient gem of Tamil literature by Ilango Adigal), S.S. Vaasan's *Mangamma Sabadham* and *Avvaiyaar*, Sivaji Ganesan's historicals and mythologicals – were, like *Iruvar*, unique to the region, as are later works like Kamal Haasan's *Thevar Magan* (which was set in an all-too-generic North Indian village in its remake *Viraasat*) or what his up-coming *Virumaandi* promises to be.

Iruvar appears influenced by other sources just as Tamil cinema has frequently been. Aishwarya Rai first plays the short-lived wife of Anandan, then portrays a starlet who floors him because she looks exactly like the wife, and Anandan's obsessive attachment to her seems very much like James Stewart's obsession for the second Kim Novak (who looks exactly like the first Kim Novak character) in Alfred Hitchcock's *Vertigo*. This sort of appropriation isn't particularly Tamilian – it's Indian – but the remakes sometimes redeem themselves with other virtues, like how *Chase a Crooked Shadow* became the stylish musical bonanza *Pudhiya Paravai*.

The title of *Iruvar* is itself reminiscent of AVM's *Naam Iruvar* – a patriotic, if not exactly political, film of the forties whose success did much to veer Tamil cinema away from the mythologicals and the historicals into social themes. Before *Naam Iruvar*, save the odd

Sevasadanam or *Thyagabhoomi*, most movies – *Keechaka Vadham* (the first Tamil silent film), *Meenakshi Kalyaanam*, *Gajendra Moksham*, *Kalidas* (the first Tamil talkie) – were based on epics and myths. Only later did the movies – from C.N. Annadurai's *Velaikkaari* to Durai's *Pasi* (shot amidst the slums of Madras) to Balu Mahendra's *Veedu* – begin reflecting the world around. This transition can be glimpsed in *Iruvar*, in the segments that show the shooting of Anandan's films which progress from *raja-rani* milieus to contemporary society.

Iruvar has a breathtaking style that brings to mind Tamil cinema, both old and new. The film is a passage through time, and an early song sequence showing Anandan – this name is itself that of a small-time hero of the fifties and the sixties who starred in the likes of *Vijayapuri Veeran* and *Veerathirumagan* – romancing his lady is shot in black and white, with the elaborately ornamental wipes found in films of the *Ambikapathi* period. Vairamuthu's lyrics here incorporate suitably chaste Tamil words, A.R. Rahman's heavily Carnatic style music appropriates the characteristics of early composers like G. Ramanathan and S.V. Venkataraman, and this song is sung by Unnikrishnan and Bombay Jayashree. (While the former's sweetly melodious voice isn't exactly a fit with the robust male timbres of the time, say, that of M.K. Thyagaraja Bhagavathar, the latter suitably approximates the heavy voice of a P. Leela or an M.L. Vasanthakumari.)

The setting of *Iruvar* then changes to the sixties and we see studio sets, a heroine imitating Saroja Devi's curvaceous dance moves, a tune befitting the Viswanathan-Ramamurthy era, and a soprano voice like that of P. Sushila. The vocal characteristics of T.M. Soundararajan, the star male playback singer of this period, are imbibed for the number *aayirathil naan oruvan* – a nod to *Aayirathil Oruvan*, an MGR hit – and the lyrics here go *ini ezhugnaayiru ezhuga indha irul koottangal ozhiga*, a reference to the Rising Sun (the DMK party's symbol to this day) dispelling the surrounding darkness.

We then move to the modern period, expecting a song in the style of Ilayaraja, but what we get is a jazz-era piece that would fit right into The Cotton Club, and this incongruousness is also something that's a part of Tamil cinema, where set pieces are simply about entertainment, without much regard to period detail. What's important, however, is that each of these time periods and the corresponding sequences are stunningly shot and beautifully designed. This is very much true of today's Tamil cinema – even the most routine potboiler is technically top-notch, and technicians from the industry are much in demand all over India.

Iruvar is unforgettable for the bigness of its canvas – from desert ranges to waterfalls, from elaborate sets that recreate a period to huge contemporary buildings that serve as the backdrop for political action. Tamil, and indeed Indian, cinema has always been larger than life, but bigness – not just in terms of remuneration, like the unheard-of one lakh rupees that was paid to get theatre star K.B. Sundarambal to do *Nandanar*, but in terms of scale – has also been a part of the industry right from the films of S.S. Vaasan, the Cecil B. De Mille of India.

Vaasan's Gemini Studios – the one with the famous logo of the twins blowing bugles – churned out massive-scale entertainments like *Balanaagamma*, *Aboorva Sagothարargal*, *Vanjikottai Vaaliban*, and especially *Chandralekha*, with its climactic drum dance featuring hundreds of extras. The sixties saw the slew of gargantuan mythologicals and historicals with technicolour that sometimes hurt the eye, the eighties saw the films of T. Rajendar, a multi-tasking maverick whose grandiose sets were often major attractions, and today, a Shankar is known for his large-scale successes filled with special effects.

Iruvar stars Tabu and Aishwarya Rai, both actresses of fair complexion who do not know a word of Tamil. (The two would co-star again in Rajeev Menon's *Kandukondain Kandukondain*.) This occasionally happened earlier, when Radha Saluja appeared in a series of hits opposite MGR or when Bharatiraja tried to palm off the *pucca*-Punjabi-looking Rati Agnihotri as a Tamil Nadu villager in *Pudhiya Vaarppugal*, but it's after Khushboo stormed Chennai and blazed a trail of success that northern heroines (Simran, Jyothika, Kiran) have become a must in Tamil films.

The heroes of *Iruvar*, interestingly, aren't stars but actors, which is again something occasionally found in Tamil cinema. The male stars, the top heroes, are usually worshipped like Gods, but there has always been a place for unconventional leads, like Vijayan in the seventies, who appeared in *Udhiri Pookkal* and *Niram Maaraadha Pookkal*.

Iruvar reflects realism – the Malayali flavour of Mohanlal's Tamil underscored the fact that MGR himself was a Malayali – and this is something Tamil cinema has increasingly embraced, more so since the entry of Bharatiraja. The latter, with his debut in *16 Vayadhinile*, moved films out of the studios and into villages to bring rustic sights and sounds like never before. He also tackled several real issues – *Vedham Pudhidhu* dealt with the caste system, *Pudhumai Penn* was about the position of women in society – and earlier creators like Jayakanthan have explored real (as opposed to melodramatic) relationships in films like *Sila Nerangalil Sila Manidhargal*.

Another aspect of the realism in *Iruvar* is found in the absence of a separate comedy track, and today even the odd commercial effort like *Kaakha Kaakha* or *Pithamagan* has done away with the intended-for-laughs insertions that have been integral to Tamil cinema from the days of N.S. Krishnan and T.A. Madhuram. Most mainstream movies, of course, still have comedy tracks, but even there you have funny men, like the socially responsible Vivek, who try to infuse some semblance of reality into their wisecracks.

Iruvar was a good film that met with a pathetic response at the box office, a phenomenon all too true of Tamil cinema. Anything that's too different is usually rejected by the masses, as Kamal Haasan recently discovered with *Anbe Sivam* and Mani Ratnam himself found with his last release *Kannathil Muthamittaal*.

However, *Iruvar* won other wars, with invitations to film festivals around the world – like the 51st Locarno International Film Festival 1998 – much like *Nayakan* was screened at Toronto. Quality Tamil cinema that doesn't work locally today often finds fame elsewhere — *Hey Ram*, for instance, became part of a course on Indian cinema at the University of Iowa.

Iruvar, finally, represents something positive – the ambition of current Tamil cinema. Tamil films have always been ambitious, but mostly in terms of scope and scale. Today, the ambition is more about themes, about risks. A director like Bala is not only able to get away with his utterly morbid scenarios in *Sethu*, *Nandha* and *Pithamagan*, he also lands top heroes like Vikram and Suriya to participate in them. Mani Ratnam himself, after all-out commercial fare like *Agni Natchatiram* and *Thirudaa Thirudaa*, has become more artistically ambitious with the much-lauded likes of *Bombay* and *Kannathil Muthamittaal*.

Tamil cinema will always remain slave to the box office, but even in the midst of mere masala, there is enough scope for art and craft, which is what is exemplified by Mani Ratnam and his *Iruvar*.

Turtles and antelopes

S. THEODORE BASKARAN

THE year, 1965. The sun had gone down and an early moon dimly lit the Santhome beach in Madras. There were no one else on the beach. Thilaka and I were sitting there wondering if it was time to leave when we heard the sound of sand being shovelled. Turning back we saw behind us what appeared to be a dark mound a few metres away. It took only a few seconds to recognize the shovelling movement of the flippers of a sea turtle. Olive Ridley to be specific. We got up and squatted close watching it prepare its nest. That was one of my early introductions to the wildlife of Chennai.

Only a few cities are as blessed as Chennai is with varied geographical features – rivers, sea front, hills, lakes, backwaters, swamps and an estuary. And few have squandered such a heritage as we have done in a frenzied and unbalanced urbanization.

When the British traders began building a fort near the village Madarasapatinam in 1639, thereby taking the first step towards founding the city of Madras, the area was replete with wildlife. Marshes stretched along the seacoast. The British soldiers often set out of the fort to shoot waterfowl that congregated in the marshes. The

Quibble Island, with its expanses of swamp and marshes attracting hordes of waterfowl like snipe and curlews, was a favourite hunting ground for the British. Along the coast were vast areas of tropical dry evergreen forest in which antelopes roamed. Two rivers, the Adyar and the Coovum, meandered close by. And there was this long sea front that the British artistes celebrated through their etchings. The landscape was dotted with lakes of varied sizes. Decades later, when the British officers were engaged in land survey in 1800, they reported sighting tigers in Vandalur hills, just 40 km from the fort.

The picture we have now is very different. A modern factory, sprawling under the shadow of Vandalur hills, is busy producing cars and the nearest spot where tigers can be found is the Mudumalai sanctuary, 600 km away, where a mere twenty-five lead a precarious existence. The lakes survive only as names of townships. Most of the tidal mud flats and creeks have been reclaimed by land hungry urbanites and converted into colonies such as Foreshore estate. The beach has been vandalized and buildings have come up close to the sea. The rivers have been defiled beyond recognition and the hills blasted out of shape to produce concrete. The estuary has been encroached upon and constricted out of its distinctiveness as a habitat.

But a patch of coastal scrub jungle, a mere 271 ha, has survived, albeit in a degenerate form and is now a national park. In 1947 it was a 400 ha expanse but parts of this prime forest was allotted to various institutions and over the years it has shrunk to what it is now. The Guindy Deer Park is a link with the ecological past of the city and provides an idea of the heritage lost. This is one of the last holds of the endangered antelope that is exclusive to India, the blackbuck. It is the fastest animal in India, capable of running fifteen kilometres at a stretch keeping an average of 70 km/h and at times peaking at an astonishing 90 km/h. Once plentiful in the plains, the blackbuck is now seen only in a few protected areas like the Point Calimere Sanctuary in Nagapattinam district and in the Thengumarada forests in Erode district.

The park is also home to spotted deer but these are not endemic to the jungle; they have been introduced and in time have flourished. The park has quite a few other mammals such as the jackal, Indian hare and monitor lizard. It is also home to a variety of reptiles, including the star tortoise. More than a hundred varieties of birds, migrant and residents, can be spotted in the park. Among the noteworthy are the green-billed malkoha, a resident cuckoo that builds its own nest and the forest wagtail, a migrant bird of the size of a sparrow with zebra markings on its grey body. As a sanctuary for wild animals and as a laboratory for researchers, the importance of this park is increasingly being recognized.

In the early 1970s, enthused by the initial waves of conservation efforts, a group of us set out to prepare a checklist of birds of the Guindy Deer Park. The red-winged cuckoo, a migrant that visits the wooded part of the city, is easily spotted. It breeds in North East India and migrates South. My friend and fellow twitcher 10-volume Narayanaswamy recorded the presence of this cuckoo in Guindy and surprised even a seasoned birder like M. Krishnan. You might wonder about the prefix to his name. When the other birders barely managed to posses a copy of Salim Ali's *Book of Indian Birds*, Narayanaswamy was the proud owner of all the 10 volumes of the newly released *Handbook of the Birds of India and Pakistan* by Salim Ali and Dillon Ripley. Whence the identity.

The Guindy Park also played a crucial role in conservation education. It was here that quite a few wildlife enthusiasts honed their concern, began their life-long involvement with wildlife and now contribute to the cause of conservation in India. R. Sukumar, Chairman of Asian Elephant Specialist group of IUCN, Shantharam who gave up a career as a chartered accountant to become an ornithologist and Ravi Chellam, India's lion man, now with the UNDP, are some of the names I can think of.

Though most of the swampy areas of the city have given way to residential colonies, the Adyar estuary survived, till recently. An estuary, where the fresh water of the river meets the brackish water of the sea, is a unique and fragile ecosystem, representing a habitat between the land and the sea. It presents a transitional condition that is never static. The important feature of this environment is the constant change of mixture of salt and fresh-water. It is dominated by fine sedimentary material, taken into the estuary by the tidal flow and this forms the mud flats. The ebb and flow of the tidal currents work on the soil and make it a nursery of many aquatic creatures. During low tide, a vast area of the riverbed is bared and a host of wading birds feed on the tiny crabs and other small creatures.

In the migratory season, waterfowl of different varieties, thousands of sandpipers and shanks, long-legged waders, flock to this feeding ground. The little stint, a tiny, winter visitor, comes all the way from Eastern Europe and remains till the end of March. The flamingos that used to visit the estuary have their breeding grounds in the Rann of Kutch. They can also be seen in Thada lake on the outskirts of the city. Rare plants like mangroves bordered the estuary. In fact, some remnants of these mangroves can still be seen on the Theosophical Society side.

The Theosophical Society campus sustains a considerable bird population. The variety of trees, both indigenous and exotic (including the two baobab trees) attracts migrants and resident birds. On my evening walks, in addition to celebrities like paradise flycatchers, I have sighted star-tortoise moving unhurriedly across the path. The howl of jackals after sunset seems to celebrate the protection they enjoy on the campus.

While developing the city, the citizens and administration seem to have completely ignored the presence of the sea front. Buildings have been erected too close to the sea and encroachments of various size have been allowed to grow. Long stretches of the beach are virtual latrines. The school of dolphins that shows up near the coast spasmodically goes unnoticed. Two kinds of dolphins can easily be sighted in the sea off Chennai: the bottle-nosed dolphin and the hump-backed. Madras Yacht Club members tell me that schools of the latter variety are seen more often around Chennai. Though there has been no record of whale sighting in recent years, in 1890 a sperm whale was washed ashore on the coast of Chennai, and the skull is on display in the Madras museum. The occasional whale shark that gets beached and appears as news item is an indication of what the sea contains in the shape of life forms.

It is only in recent decades that the need to conserve and care for our wildlife heritage has been articulated in Madras city. In the forties and fifties, M. Krishnan, one of the early conservationists, was ploughing a lonely furrow by writing on wildlife, first in Tamil and later prolifically in English. The burden of his song was that we should recognize animals, birds, rivers and hills as our heritage. His column 'Southern Diary' in *The Illustrated Weekly* often carried pieces on the wildlife of the city. He inspired many wildlife enthusiasts. Harry Miller, writing in *The Indian Express* drew people's attention to reptiles and birds and kindled the light in many budding wildlife photographers.

The founding of the Snake Park in Chennai in 1969, largely due to the efforts of Romulus Whitaker, with assistance from the World Wildlife Fund, was a landmark in the conservation movement in this part of the country. Ignorance about snakes, compounded by superstition, destruction of their habitats and a boom in the snakeskin industry has spelt disaster for the reptiles. In the late 1950s, one tannery near Madras was curing five to ten thousands snake skins daily. In addition to the legal steps taken by the government, protection also came in the form of a public conscious of wildlife. A key effort of the snake park was to educate the public and to encourage research on Indian herpetofauna. In this task, the services of the Irula tribals were harnessed and their traditional knowledge put into use in conservation work. More important, the park became a training ground for youngsters interested in wildlife and some of them, such as Shekhar Dattatri who grew to be a wildlife filmmaker and Satish Bhaskar who blossomed into an expert on turtles made a career of their interest.

The surge of enthusiasm for wildlife conservation that swept the country in the early seventies had its impact on Chennai. In 1970, Romulus Whitaker, then managing the Madras Snake Park, was living by the sea and observed the decimation that the sea turtles were being subjected to. Along with Satish Bhaskar and Jean Delouche, he initiated steps to save the turtles. With a group of volunteers, he organized what came to be known as 'turtle walks'. During nesting season volunteers walked along the beach at night covering the area from Marina to Kalpakkam and collected the eggs.

According to their estimate about 14,000 Olive Ridley turtles came to the Chennai beaches for nesting. Whitaker and his team persuaded National and Grindlays Bank to provide a space in Injambakam, where a makeshift hatchery was set up and the eggs were buried under sand to hatch. In 1982, the WWF took up and continued the hatchery programme. Soon the Forest Department stepped in and set up three more hatcheries. Whitaker demonstrated what could be done with very little resource and a strong belief in the cause. He was subsequently to prove the same point with regard to crocodiles. Later, Chandy Abraham and Karthik Shankar formed the Students' Sea Turtle Conservation Network and carried on the work. Now, Murugavel of the Trust for Restoration of Ecology and Environment (TREE) and other volunteers continue turtle walks. In addition to helping the turtles, these walks continue to win new converts to the cause of conservation in Chennai.

In 1978, about 16 wildlife enthusiasts of the city led by Vivek Kunte, joined and formed the Madras Naturalist Society. To begin with there were two concerns that brought them together: one was the Adyar estuary and the other, the Guindy Deer Park. One of their first activities was to carry out a census of the blackbuck and chital population of the park. In 1980, the members took Salim Ali to the estuary to give him an idea of its bird wealth. In 1982, a survey of the Madras beach from Ennore to Covalam was done. Its quarterly journal *Blackbuck*, begun in 1983, has established itself as a reputed publication providing a forum for many non-professionals to document their observations on wildlife. With 300 members, of whom 180 are for life, the MNS has the capability to serve as an enlightened voice for the city's natural heritage.

Even now, in the new millennium, there are some pockets of greenery in the city that serve as wildlife habitats – the Theosophical Society, the Indian Institute of Technology, Anna University, the museum and Women's Christian College. In addition to the trees there, these 'green spaces' sustain a variety of birds like the golden backed woodpecker and spotted owlets; there are also mammals – toddy cat, squirrels, flying foxes and mongooses. Small ponds inside the city attract pond herons and the white-breasted kingfisher. Inside the IIT Madras campus is a roosting site for open-bill storks and white ibis. A few years ago I lived in a house on Commander-in-Chief road where a family of mongooses were regular visitors to our garden.

One threat to wildlife in the city is the growing population of stray dogs. The corporation has stopped its programme of elimination of strays and they have multiplied in the thousands. In the Guindy Deer Park and the IIT campus, they prey on the fawns of chital and blackbuck, steeply bringing down their numbers. Along the beach, the strays smell out turtle nests and feed on the eggs. This problem is yet to be addressed.

Though Chennai appears to be a city of trees from the air, much of the tree cover has gone. The evergreen indigenous trees like the banyan, peepal, neem, mango, and pungamia, tamarind and wood apple can be seen only in some parts of the city. In recent decades we also observe a change in the kind of trees that are planted. Exotics, which are small in spread and weak in the trunk, are favoured. For instance, the gulmohar sheds its leaves in summer, when we need shade most. Instead, there is need to propagate indigenous varieties such as neem and peepal. The people's obsession with coconut palms militates against providing a proper green cover. Though hardly anyone harvests coconuts from the trees planted in their houses, the tree remains popular. The concretizing of pavements has spelt death for the trees. The tree trunk is covered all around, as if it was a lamp post and eventually the tree dies. There has been no sustained tree-growing programme in the city.

But nothing is more symbolic of the utter disregard for wildlife heritage as the destruction of the Adyar estuary. Biologists point to the estuaries as the most productive natural habitats of the world. The food web here is complicated and so the area invites specialized feeders. It takes eons to shape an estuary and we have ruined it overnight by deciding to dredge it, preparatory to setting up a boathouse. If only the sanctuary had been given protection it would have attracted a lot more tourists – if that were the purpose – than a few boats will ever do. And we would have had a heritage intact.

The environmental degradation of Chennai is also indicated in many other ways. Water shortage is one. All the wetlands in the city have been reclaimed and the water resources neglected. The lakes at Nungambakkam and Vyasarpadi have been overwhelmed by urban sprawl. This process of destroying wetlands, our main life-support system, continues. The marshes near Foreshore Estate in Santhome are getting filled up. The latest in the list is Pallikaranai swamp, a vast stretch of marshy wetland adjoining Velacherry in South Madras, which is getting filled up with the garbage of the city. As wetlands and lakes shrink inexorably, the water table falls drastically and subterranean aquifers get depleted.

The bird population, which is a good indicator of the ecological health of any area, has come down drastically. One sees less and less of them both in the ground and in the sky. In the seventies, in Besant Nagar, we used to watch a pair of white-bellied sea eagle soar along the sea front. The birders knew that the pair nested inside the Theosophical Society. They are no more to be seen.

Still, even today Chennai has a considerable bird population. We often sight the golden oriole in the gulmohar tree in our house. There are occasional white-headed babblers and drogues that visit us. The tailor-birds and bulbuls are always there. A crimson-throated barbet shows up sometimes. You would hear pied-wagtails perched on water tanks in the terrace of flat complexes. In the evenings we see batches of mynas fly overhead to their roosting spot for the night. Flocks of rose-ringed parakeets dash across as if they have just remembered an important appointment. The western sky grows deep pink and from their many roosting spots in the city come night herons, on leisurely wing bets, silhouetted against the crimson backdrop. They are flying towards their feeding ground for the night... the backwaters of Muttukadu? There they will feed till daybreak when the golden oriole starts calling from the Gulmohar tree, announcing another day.

Curdrice cricket

V. RAMNARAYAN

NOT long ago, four Chennai cricketers were barred from playing any further games for the season, following unacceptably aggressive on-field behaviour during a league match. Their 'sledging' prowess would have put the worst excesses of the Australian Test team to shame. All four suspended players belonged to the fielding side, the umpire who reported the incident to the cricket association finding the opponents innocent of any misdemeanour. 'They were perhaps cleverer than those who got caught,' the cynics said. 'Chances are that they too mouthed obscenities, insulted the opposition, and questioned their parentage; only they did it out of the umpires' hearing, to go by the general trend of behaviour on our cricket grounds.'

What a far cry this scene is from Madras cricket of yore. Just to give you an idea of the kind of spirit that pervaded the game as it was played here in the fifties and sixties, even the seventies, let's join the action in the first ball of a limited over match back in the sixties. The new ball bowler K.S.S. Mani is known for movement and intelligent variation rather than speed. The batsman is R. Vijayaraghavan, an entertaining stroke-maker. To 'Viji', if a ball is there to be hit, it is meant to be hit, even if it is the first ball of a match. Mani's first delivery is an inswinging half volley, and Viji flicks it imperiously over square leg for six. The crowd is on its feet, but look at Mani's reaction. He runs to the batsman and pats him on his back, shouting, 'Great shot da, Viji.' Though such extreme acts of sportsmanship were not a daily occurrence, most of the cricket of the time was played in a spirit of friendly combat.

Cricket was initially an elitist pursuit, learned originally from the British by the landed gentry and educated upper crust and then percolating to the middle class. It was Buchi Babu Nayudu, a dubash well-versed in the ways of the ruling British at the turn of the century, who first assembled an Indian outfit capable of beating the 'European' at his own game. Soon the game spread far and wide in Madras – from Purasawalkam to Perambur, Triplicane to Mylapore and beyond, with caste Hindus and Anglo-Indians the most prominent practitioners of the game.

'Curdrice cricketers' was the epithet still reserved for Madras cricketers of my time, especially of the Brahmin variety (who probably form a substantial percentage of the cricket playing population of the city even today), though the demographics of the game was gradually changing, with many of the Anglo-Indians leaving India, and more and more of the 'backward communities' taking to the game with each succeeding generation. It was a sarcastic reference to the soporific effect of the staple diet of the majority back then. We were said to lack the steel for stern battle, our artistry and skills no match to the aggression of cricketers elsewhere.

Brilliant strokemakers and spin bowlers in local cricket, we were considered no-hopers when it came to locking horns with the more robust if less stylish combatants from Delhi or Bombay. Fielding was at best an unavoidable nuisance and the slips the preserve of seniors, with the babies of the team banished to the distant outposts of long leg and third man. Fast bowling was too close to real work, left best in the hands of those endowed with more brawn than brain.

League cricket then was relatively informal. There was no registration of players by the clubs, and you could walk in a few minutes before the toss and join the eleven. There was much banter and fielders and batsmen often traded jokes or gossip, with the umpires sometimes joining in. The action rarely approached the frenetic and the accent was invariably on style rather than substance. The spinner who did not turn the ball and the batsman of dour defence or crude power were treated with contempt by all these different constituents of the game in my youth. To give you an idea of the cricketing values of the period, I – as an off spinner – was not infrequently warned by umpires that all my appeals would be refused unless I flighted the ball! To them, how you bowled was more important than taking wickets.

On most grounds, the shade of a large tree served as the dressing room and facilities were generally primitive. Lunch involved a hurried dash to Ratna Café, Udipi Sukha Nivas, Shanti Vihar, Udipi Home or Dasprakash and back, depending on the venue of the match. The effects of the blazing sun were countered by glasses of unboiled, unfiltered and often multihued water stored in mud pots or brought in buckets that resembled relics dug out by archaeological expeditions.

Most Madras cricketers were unable to afford high quality gear. In fact, you needed contacts abroad or access to visiting Test cricketers to buy bats and other gear from them at fancy prices. A Gunn and Moore, Gray Nicolls or Autograph bat could cost upwards of a hundred rupees and that was a lot of money for the average cricketer. The gloves, leg guards and shoes worn by most of us often performed a psychological rather than protective role. At the lower levels of cricket it was not unusual for batsmen to wear a single leg guard rather than a pair because that was all the team could afford. The bats could be handcrafted things of beauty, but they did not possess the carry of contemporary bats that can send a top edge out of the ground.

Despite these constraints or possibly because of them – for they served to make playing cricket seem an adventure, a privilege earned by the worthy, not something handed to you on a platter as it is today – the enthusiasm for the game was plentiful and infectious among players and spectators alike, not to mention the men behind the scenes like club secretaries, scorers and markers. Of humour, there was never any shortage and the spirit of competition was always softened by a sense of camaraderie that went beyond team loyalties.

Cricket was an indispensable part of growing up in sleepy Madras of the 1950s and 1960s. Everywhere in the city, there were cricket-mad children, their fancy fed by radio commentary and newspaper reports, and the occasional visit to the cricket ground to watch their local heroes. In most houses with sizable compounds, siblings, cousins and their neighbourhood friends played much of their cricket within the four walls of their homes. We had charcoal stumps drawn on a number of walls in the compound, every corridor and hallway was a makeshift ground when it was too hot outside, there were three or four pitches within the compound that we kids levelled and rolled – even had cowdung sprayed by our helpful domestic staff – but for most of us the crowning glory was a vast 'ground' nearby, empty plots of land still to be swallowed by residential buildings.

Usually, the wicket was a beauty, levelled by humans and cattle using them as shortcuts from one street to another. The ground was often manicured by grazing buffaloes, which seemed to equal the human population of the streets we lived on.

Only when it rained did the playing surface pose problems, challenging the technique and courage of the barefoot batsmen, while transforming military medium pacers into demon fast bowlers. The hoofmarks of the buffaloes on wet soil hardened into dangerous ridges from which the ball reared up steeply. Batting then became largely a matter of survival of the luckiest.

There were countless such private grounds which the young cricketers simply entered one day and occupied, so to speak, until the Rip Van Winkle who owned the plot woke up suddenly to build his dream house, in the process shattering the dreams of many prospective Prasannas and Venkataraghavans, Pataudis and Bordes. Only for the dreams to be resumed in technicolour as soon as the intrepid young cricket warriors conquered their next new territory.

Cricket did not stop even in the classroom, where boys played 'book cricket', by opening pages at random and affixing runs or dismissals to the two imaginary batsmen – they could be Mankad and Roy in one generation and Gavaskar and Viswanath the next. If for example you opened page 54, the second digit was the reference point for the scorekeeping, and the batsman got four runs (or two, under a different set of rules), if the page number ended in a zero, the batsman was declared out and so on.

In my extended family, we invented our own brand of home cricket, an ingenious adaptation of the bagatelle board in which we gave cricket values to the various points on the board. 150 was six runs, 125 was four, LTP was bowled, 75 was two runs, 90 three, and we had different positions for different kinds of dismissals, caught, lbw, stumped, run out, even hit wicket. A skilful player, experienced in steering the little steel ball bearings we used for marbles, could make his team score 300-400 runs if he held his nerve, and score those runs pretty rapidly. It provided perverse pleasure to make Laker and Lock or Desai and Surendranath score centuries after the top order had failed.

Madras cricket of those days had its share of characters. P.R. Sundaram, a first rate fast medium bowler and an entertaining wielder of the long handle, was also one of the funniest men seen on a cricket field. He kept up a fairly constant chatter on the field, and was not above laughing at an umpire after he had given a dubious decision. He once informed an official after he had lifted his finger in response to his own loud appeal, that the poor batsman had not played the ball on its way to the wicketkeeper. On another occasion, he bowled a googly as his opening delivery of the match and laughed with his arms akimbo at the batsman who had been bowled shouldering arms.

Some others raised a laugh without intending to. There was 'Kulla Kitta' Krishnamurthy, who opened the innings for Crom-Best Recreation Club, one of numerous short statured players known by that nickname over the years, who, dismissed off the first ball of a match once, told the incoming batsman as they crossed: 'Be careful. He moves the ball both ways.' 'Dochu' Duraiswami bowled a series of full tosses in a junior match at the Central College ground in Bangalore and later declared to his teammates: 'I have never bowled on a turf wicket before.'

Opening batsman Balu sat up all night reading Don Bradman's 'The Art of Cricket' with every intention of putting precept into practice, only to be run out first ball next morning, his partner's straight drive brushing the bowler's fingers on the way to the stumps, and catching him out of the crease! 'Clubby' Clubwalla was another popular character whom the crowds loved to boo, for his slow batting and fascinating contortions whether batting at the top of the order or bowling his alleged off spin with a most complicated action. He was a stonewaller par excellence who once made 37 runs in a whole day of batting.

There were other unforgettable characters. Probably the best known was K.S. Kannan, the veteran all-rounder who became one of the best-loved coaches of the state, more famous for his original English than his undeniable cricket skills. For a man who was fluent in Tamil, his mother tongue, but could barely pass muster in English, he loved expressing himself in the Queen's language, with invariably hilarious results. 'Give me the ball to him,' he would tell one of his wards, and 'ask me to pad up one batsman.' 'Thanking you, yours faithfully, K.S. Kannan,' were the famous last words of a speech he made at a school function.

In recent years, the stylish right hand batsman T.E. Srinivasan was famous for his wit and eccentric behaviour. On an Australian tour, his only one, T.E. allegedly told a local press reporter, 'Tell Dennis Lillee T.E. has arrived.' On the same tour he persuaded a security official at a Test match to warn innocent Yashpal Sharma that he would be arrested if he continued to stare at the ladies through his binoculars. Yashpal's panic and the resultant roar of laughter from the Indian dressing room caused a stoppage in the middle as the batsman Gavaskar drew away annoyed by the disturbance.

League matches often attracted crowds in excess of a thousand and the 30-overs a side Sport & Pastime (later *The Hindu*) Trophy final invariably drew five or six thousand spectators. Many finals were played at the Marina ground on the Beach Road, now Kamarajar Salai, which wore a festive appearance on such occasions, with every seat in the gallery taken, every treeshade occupied and dozens of cars and scooters parked on Beach Road, providing a vantage view of the match from just beyond a low wall. If you were patrolling the boundary line, you could eavesdrop on the most knowledgeable cricket conversations among spectators who knew not only the finer points of the game but also the relative merits of all the league teams and their players backwards. You could even receive some useful advice gratis, but God save you if you misfielded or dropped a catch!

Devoted spectators sometimes went from ground to ground watching more than one match in a single day. 'IOB 73 for 4 at Viveka, State Bank 100 for no loss at Marina, Jolly Rovers 82 for 2 at Pachaiyappa's,' one of them, a league cricket fanatic of many years' standing, would announce even before parking his scooter. Quickly collecting the scores at this new venue, he would troop off to provide similar information to players at another ground anxious to learn how the competition was faring elsewhere. Today, coaches and managers carry cell phones and information is exchanged instantly and effortlessly by all the protagonists involved in the chase for match points.

A Ranji trophy match between Tamil Nadu and Karnataka or Hyderabad could draw a crowd of 20,000-30,000 paying spectators. A match at Chepauk, with all its historic association with the 'Pongal' match of yore, was a most enjoyable spectacle, watched by somnolent vacationers seated under the trees surrounding the ground. That was before the concrete cauldron that today effectively reduces cricketers to dehydrated invalids in a matter of hours came to dominate the landscape.

It was an occasion to pack your *puliyodarai* and *thair sadam* and set out on a day-long excursion to catch up with old friends, and in their company, dissect the doings of the protagonists of the drama being enacted before you, to applaud or barrack bowlers, batsmen and fielders.

Madras crowds are not only knowledgeable but generally hard-to-please as well. They will never accept Anil Kumble as a better bowler than their own V.V. Kumar, a wrist spinner in the orthodox mould unlike the Karnataka express googly specialist. Gundappa Viswanath of the steely wrists and the nonchalant artistry ranks higher with them than Sunil Gavaskar, for all the Little Master's achievements and peerless technique.

Oldtimers even today experience goosebumps when they recall a magnificent innings of 215 played at Chepauk by the Ceylon stylist Sathasivam in 1940. According to many, no better innings has ever been played at Chepauk. But post-War cricket enthusiasts rate G.R. Viswanath's unbeaten 97 against West Indies in January 1975 as the greatest innings in living memory, better than the best Gavaskar and Tendulkar knocks played at the same venue – and there have been plenty of those at Chepauk. The Triplicane crowds still wax lyrical about E.A.S. Prasanna's deadly spell in 1969, when he had Australia reeling at 24 for 6, and will be the first to admit that their own local hero Venkataraghavan could not have hoped to equal the magic of that afternoon.

That is the one feature of the Madras crowd that you will rarely find elsewhere in India – the ability to transcend regional, even national bias to appreciate true sporting endeavour and artistry. This sportsmanship was never more in evidence than when the Pakistanis under Wasim Akram did a victory lap at the end of a pulsating match India almost won in 1999. I remember the drama of that afternoon as though it happened yesterday. The crowd had been roaring its approval all morning as Tendulkar led an incredible assault on the rival bowling, supported by the gallant Nayan Mongia. Unfortunately, with victory seemingly within easy reach, Sachin succumbed to the strain of the painful back injury he had been carrying throughout the innings, and soon it was all over for India.

There was a stunned silence, as if the huge crowd was still waiting for a signal from the small but significant saffron brigade in the stands that had been shouting anti-Pakistan slogans on the last day of the match (Bal Thackeray had earlier called for a ban on the tour). Like many others in the pavilion terrace, I looked back anxiously at the leader of the group, who, after what seemed like an interminable wait, gave the thumbs up to his followers. They burst into applause and the rest of the stadium joined in thunderous ovation as the victors did their triumphant march around the ground. It was a moment to make every Indian proud.

This wonderful spectator support for cricket is bolstered by passionate corporate enthusiasm for the game. Chennai is the home of a uniquely powerful form of industry-institution cooperation to promote sport, especially cricket. Companies like India Cements, Chemplast Sanmar, SPIC, India Pistons, MRF and SICAL have 'adopted' colleges and spent fortunes on developing and maintaining world class cricket facilities, with superb turf wickets and practice facilities. Institutions like Southern Railway, Integral Coach factory and Sri Ramachandra Medical College also maintain similar grounds. These patrons as well as public sector banks SBI, IOB and Indian Bank have traditionally ensured the livelihood security of sportsmen by offering them jobs or professional contracts, though the banks are now no longer the safe havens they used to be. The MRF Pace Foundation, the MAC Spin Foundation and numerous private initiatives serve to supplement the coaching programmes of the Tamil Nadu Cricket Association, one of the better run cricket bodies in the country.

All these developments have helped transform the Tamil Nadu cricketer into a professional, physically and mentally tougher than his predecessors. Proof is provided by the greater frequency of the state team's appearance in the final rounds of the Ranji Trophy and the increasing number of Tamil Nadu players knocking at Test doors in recent times. Yet, like the many corporate patrons of the state's cricket, most of whom have supported it for love of the game rather than any publicity, I still enjoy the curdrice flavour of Tamil Nadu cricket that has lingered despite the march of time and hope it does not lose it altogether.

New wine in the old bottle

TIMERI N. MURARI

OHHH, how many aspersions have rained down on my home town over the years. It's been called iddliville, thayresaadamtown, sambarsuburb, dhotiville. At one time when it was known as Madras, it deserved those names. Madras might have been the capital of the vast sprawl south of the Vindhyas called Madras Presidency but it had never had any pretensions to capital lifestyles. Frankly, it was a village well into the mid-20th century.

At dusk, the town went to sleep as everyone maintained those old village habits believing that without natural light one slept, and woke before dawn for a day's healthy work. Our visitors were few and far between, and spent most of their brief stay whining about the heat and the humidity and, above all, nothing to do apart from sitting on our famous Marina beach watching the tide come in and out. We probably had a red light district but I was damned if I knew where it was, unlike notorious Bombay with its Grant Road that I'd only heard about.

No one dreamt of eating out in a restaurant, not that there were many to choose from – either a *thali* or the famous Chunking on

Mount Road. If I had dared to suggest lunch or dinner in a restaurant my grandmother would drown me in guilt. 'Why? What's wrong with my food? Isn't it good enough for you that you have to spend money to eat rice and sambar in a restaurant? Is restaurant food better than mine?' Of course not, I'd reply meekly, beaten by her logic, and settle for her excellent cooking.

Food forms one of the basis of any cultural identity and, quite rightly, we were identified by what we ate. The British had honed foody insults into a fine art. You were what you ate. The French are still the 'frogs' for their fondness for this delicacy, and it has a sharper sting than being called 'snails'. While the Germans remain 'krauts' because of their fondness for sauerkraut. Many Asians in Britain are called 'papadoms' which may reflect the old Empire's dying imagination for insults.

We Madrasis were conservative in our eating habits, and conservative as people. We were not big drinkers, that's if we could get a drink between the bouts of prohibition that came and went like a bad flu. Tandoor was a foreign word and a foreign food, and Madrasis resisted any invasion of northern Indian culinary favourites. We allowed in the biryani but slyly subverted it by making it with vegetables and changing its taste and texture. Way back then in those traditional days the first time I tasted a tandoori chicken and nibbled on a naan was in a flock-papered Indian restaurant in London.

I left my town, we couldn't call it a city back then, for a long time and returned a few years ago. It had grown up suddenly in this last decade; it became hot in more ways than just the constant heat. Today in its new *avatar* as Chennai, the city, yes it can be called that today, has leapt over centuries to become a gourmet's delight, if not a paradise. It's as if with the name change we took on a new identity, not backward looking as the ancient name suggests, as it was called that when the British christened this strip of plantain patch on the Coromandel coast as Madras.

We're a 21st century people now, welcoming exotic dishes from all over the world. You want lobster thermidor, you've got it; want steak au poivre, you've got it. You can wallow in cannelloni, spaghetti with pesto sauce, duck à la orange, enchiladas, fish and chips, couscous, tortillas, paellas and wash them down with Australian and French wines, along with Indian brands. And this is not including Korean, Japanese, Thai, Chinese, *tandoori dabbas*, Chettinad, Gujarati, Bengali restaurants and hamburgers, pizzas and chicken wings.

Sophisticates in the other metros may mutter 'So what?' but this is a quantum leap for the Madrasi. We may still consume an idli or two for breakfast but for dinner we'll dine on lamb cutlets with a delicate béarnaise sauce, washed down with a Pinot Noir or a Burgundy. Now we're harder to define as we straddle our past and the future. We're sliding somewhere in the slipstream of cultural homogeneity, trying to keep our balance in the whirlwind rush of changes.

One day we had graceful girls dancing the Bharatanatyam at weddings, now we have belly dancers at *Mehendi's*. Unbelievable, and as villagers we all crowd around to get a glimpse of this vibrating belly when we barely glimpsed a belly button in the old days. The older generation would have swooned at such sacrilege. A friend from Mumbai, however, sneered and whispered to me that belly dancing was *passé* in his city. 'In Mumbai we used to have them but no longer,' he added with somewhat of a sneer. I figured in Mumbai they had to be into lap top dancers at the city weddings or even the dancers from the Crazy Horse, and no doubt Chennai will catch up with that trend, even if a few years late.

But we're getting there, running as fast as we can. We're getting over our social and sexual inhibitions. Another friend, condemned to two weeks in Chennai and resigned to spending his evening watching television in his hotel room, made friends in a disco and spent his evenings skinny dipping in private swimming pools along the East Coast road. He was ecstatic, proclaiming Chennai was more hip than his Mumbai. It was his luck to fall into the right swimming pools which I never knew existed.

All these changes have sort of snuck up on Chennai when it was still contemplating its *masala dosai*, until one day it went to sleep to the soothing sounds of a veena and was awakened rudely by rock/pop music on Radio Mirchi, the latest FM station with non-stop music and non-stop chatter. Chennai slept, dreaming of its girls wrapped in six yards of saree – Kanjeevaram, Mysore silk, voile – and woke to find them all now in jeans and sweat shirts, racing around on their scooters with cell phones pinned to their ears instead of malipu. Not a hip-hugging saree in sight, except at weddings and even there you'll see more skimpy salwars than chaste sarees to hide their sexy south Indian figures.

Girls meet boys openly now, flashing the latest fashions in the discos that have opened up in the city hotels, five, four and three star, but like so many cinderellas and cinderfellas they have to vanish back into the city at the midnight hour as the cops don't allow the discos to remain open until dawn. They'll reappear mid-afternoon into late evening, and all weekend, coming out of the woodwork to hang out in the Ispahani Centre on Nungumbakkam High Road.

You may think that the winds of change sweeping through sleeping Madras blew in from the West, along with *Spiderman* and *Sex in the City*. Far from it. The winds, like those ancient conquerors, swept down from north of the Vindhyas. Anyone from north of that chain are Punjabis, whatever their origin or their language, even as every Southie is called a Madrasi in the North. Our invaders drifted into the town gradually, bringing with them their social habits and imposing them on us unsuspecting Madrasis. They changed the dress styles of our women for a start. Before they brought their influence into Madras, all the women dressed in demure sarees. If some of our young women took to jeans, the others discovered and embraced the salwar with enthusiasm. I don't see a saree-clad college-going girl anywhere today and even the older women working in banks, IT, or insurance, are in their uniform salwars. They all give the same reason – easier to wear, practical and not so much angst ironing a six yard saree.

Where once dinner parties were docile affairs, finishing long before midnight, our Punjabi invaders kept us up drinking until well past midnight before serving us *tandoori chicken*, *saag*, *kebabs* and *naans* as the sun rose. They changed our Deepavalis into Diwalis, a time to eat and drink, and taught us to play poker all night long while cleaning us out. They taught us *sangeet* and *mehndi* and, most blasphemous of all, introduced us to liquor at wedding receptions when all we'd ever had before was a vegetarian thali and a lime juice.

All this was infectious. Soon we Madrasis too began to include these boisterous customs into many of our weddings; admittedly not all families followed suit. The more traditional remained steadfast to the six am *muhurtham*, followed by breakfast and an evening reception, alcohol-free. I believe I now have more 'Punjabi' friends than Madrasis. They brought in their exuberance and didn't like the idea of staying at home every evening, eating home-cooked food. They ventured out into the night and soon the hotels had to have twenty-four hour coffee shops, but that wasn't enough. My friends wanted Italian and French and Spanish food to break the monotony, to escape from the city on the magic carpet of their palates to distant lands, so the city responded by opening up these escape holes to Europe and America. Punjabis flashed their money around, but we Madrasis retained our conservative spending habits.

Oh yes, we Madrasis were quite parsimonious with our money, and we still are. I know multi-millionaires who dress humbly in shirt and trousers and drive around in Hondas or Skodas although they can afford a few Mercs. Even though Nalli, the man who created the saree mega store with branches in London and LA, moves around in a Merc, he still wears his simple white dhoti and *jiba* and, whenever I see him, he hurries away from his acquisition as if in embarrassment.

Unlike their counterparts in the North, we wealthy Chennaites don't like to flaunt our wealth. It could also be to avoid the notice of the tax man but it's ingrained in the culture to keep a low and humble profile. The man sitting next to you at a *sabha* or a dinner in his dhoti and jiba could be the wealthiest in the city but you'd never guess it. But a quick glance at his wife, overloaded with gold, diamonds and rubies like a Christmas tree, will correct any first impression.

Until a decade ago, we were happy to shop in the old parts of the city – Rattan Bazaar, Flower Bazaar, Parrys Corner. They supplied the necessities, nothing fashionable or flamboyant. Or, if we craved for the 'phoren' goods there was always Burma Bazaar, a thin stream of shops flowing outside Madras port where you could buy anything from French wines to an Italian cooker.

Then something mysterious began to gradually happen in this sleepy village. A shopping mall or two popped their heads up, nervous as gophers on a prairie. Would they survive or scuttle back into their holes, defeated by the conservatism and penny-pinching Madras habits? The malls weren't the grand expanse of capitalism to be found in the US or Europe, merely three or four floors of shops. You must remember, unlike Bombay, Madras is a horizontal city, not vertical, and three or four floors of shops at one location were unheard of. It's also a city without a centre. There's no Times Square or Oxford Circus, no downtown.

The humble malls changed this. They were attractive, certainly not stunning, architecturally. They drew people in, not merely to shop but to hang out and by hanging out they shopped. Alsa Mall in Egmore was the most popular. It had a coffee shop, British Airways, Titan watches and couple of men's clothing stores. Soon malls sprang up like mushrooms in a damp cellar. Some thrived, others withered but most importantly they had arrived. And as the survivors thrived they became bolder, more stylish and the shops began to specialise in fashion, accessories, jewellery, furniture.

The most successful one today is Spencer's Plaza, the biggest shopping mall in India. Back in the old days when the British were still here, Spencer's was the biggest department store in Asia. Then a few years ago the old Spencer's mysteriously burned down and like a phoenix rising from the ashes came our new high rise Spencer's with floor upon floor of shops. We changed with the times as the city's name changed and today you can buy anything from a gold Rolex to a Sony digital camera, from designer clothes and every foreign label to Lee jeans. We may not match Mumbai with its vast range of consumer items and fashionable designer clothes but we have enough to satisfy our moderate tastes for the modern.

But the past has not lost its hold on us. The patina of modernity lies lightly on our souls, we have adapted to it to make us more accessible and acceptable to all the new breed of invaders – Punjabis, the Brits (again), Americans, French, Germans, Japanese. In the South, Bangalore has changed from its Britishness to its Punjabiness; they have even imported in their gangsters to lend it additional character. But Bangalore always had an unstable identity. A friend remarked that the Tamil and Tamilians are cohesive, and difficult to submerge in any new identity. We remain a courteous and gracious people, and have not yet picked up the abrasive habits of the North or the West. We visit our temples regularly and draw the morning kolam outside our doors, even in the new flat-style living we've adapted to.

Unlike the North we have such a strong and unshakeable belief in ourselves and our religion that we do not practise any communalism. We have kept this slate, so badly stained in so many parts of India, clean. Christian, Muslim, Jain, Sikh live among us without the dread of a riot or a pogrom. They're confident that, over the centuries, we have always treated them with respect. I admit our politicians do try to stir up hatred, and succeed from time to time especially out in the rural areas and smaller towns, but it doesn't work in this city. In that, we have resisted the north Indian animosity towards different faiths. Those remain still north of the Vindhyas.

On the surface, as you drive through the city, you may imagine we have totally discarded the saree. But walk into Nalli's or any of the new chic saree stores anytime and you'll find it crowded with women buying their sarees. From being an everyday dress it's now taken on a fashion as a formal evening attire.

We're still book lovers. Recently, a writer from Delhi came to give us a reading of his new book and though he was unknown, he was surprised to find around fifty people waiting to hear him. He remarked at the start of his talk that in Delhi he would not have even bothered to have a reading as no one would show up. After all, the South does have a much higher literacy rate than the North and this is reflected in the popularity of books, both in English and the regional languages.

The jewel in our crown is our festival season. During November and December we still have a cultural feast of music and dance which is attended by both Madrasis and visitors from all parts of India and the world. I have Indian friends in America who regularly fly over to immerse themselves in this cultural lake which renews and invigorates them for the rest of the year in their America. No other city, anywhere in India or the world, has such a cultural extravaganza annually. Over a period of 20 days 1500 musicians, singers and dancers perform in 20 venues (sabhas) around the city.

The basis of the festival is, of course, to celebrate Carnatic music but we also have dancers and musicians from all over India vying to be included in this cultural orgy. The programmes begin nearly at dawn and finish only around midnight, and the sabhas are packed. And if you think it's only the old attending these concerts, think again. I've seen eight and ten year old children sitting still as rocks for three to four hours listening to classical music and keeping the beat. They might then go out and listen to their MTV but deep down they still retain their cultural roots through their music and dance. What other city can offer its people such a deep cultural and traditional mooring?

Cities retain their characters, no matter who invades them, and you can sniff it in the air. New York smells of the manic infectious energy, London of the staid and historical stability, Paris of possible romance and beauty. The Madras air, beneath the new odours of Chanel and pesto sauces, and even its name change, is still replete with odours of *sambar* and *rasam* and, more significant, is soaked in culture and old traditions.

Madras in words

SHREEKUMAR VARMA

A net surfer recently wrote: 'I live in Denver, Colorado. I met a padre from a local church in our gym. We swim in the same pool. He once asked me about the name Madras. He thought it came about because the British used this town to lock up all those who revolted against them. They called them Mad Rascals, in short Mad-Ras.'

There is another story with a similar twist. The British were amused by the fact that Vekatappa Naik could be crazy enough to gift away so much land to Francis Day (to build Fort St. George), asking in return only that it be named after his father Chennappa Naik (hence, Chennappattinam and then Chennai). So they called him the Mad Rasa, or the mad king. This single story explains both names, Madras and Chennai.

Someone else claims the name originated from Madri, wife of Pandu, official father of the Pandavas in the *Mahabharatha*. Madri was the mother of Nakula and Sahadeva, and is supposed to have come from this part of the country.

That's the trouble with Madras, or any other city which has great spurts of history with ambiguous linkages. I once wrote in my Sunday column that the later White Madras is available to the historian, but not the period before that. Chunks of native history before the English settlement have been virtually lost in romance and myth. Given the Indian penchant for invoking and revering legends, that early history can hardly be reclaimed with any acceptable degree of objectivity.

Historian S. Muthiah – sometimes referred to as 'Mr. Madras' for his passionate interest in the city's history and heritage – picked up my lament and agreed whole-heartedly in his own column. He himself is, however, on an endless investigative spree, unearthing facts and fables that might help to patch up a forgotten fabric. There are, in fact, pockets in the metropolitan mapwork of this rapidly modernising city that still hide a treasure or two for the chronicler. Mylapore, the temple settlement, now struggles between trade and tradition. Spirituality, music, academics and islands of extreme conservatism jostle with breathless new commerce and traffic.

There are houses in Mylapore that still breathe in an ancient past. Artefacts and valuable old manuscripts are still being dug out. Coins from Roman times were found not too long ago. Senior citizens sit on pyols, brooding over their own versions of history. Preparing for an impressionistic book on Chennai, I wondered whether it was possible to sift history from myth and, indeed, if it was even advisable.

A city like Madras (or Chennai) is as much an idea as it is a living space. It is as much the sum of impressions gathered by people through the ages as it is the daily arena of those who struggle, enjoy and work out their lives. It is a socio-political laboratory where organized living is routinely experimented with. It can change with perspective, becoming different things to different people. This is the interesting aspect of working on a city like Chennai. Each book written about the city opens up a different avenue of ideas.

I was confronted with an endless list of books already written. I had once feared there would be little reference material to work with. Now it was apparent that there was too much. And the internet being a repository (and dumping ground) of information, there was that arena to be considered as well.

Taking a few of these books at random, let us look at their scope and success. Though many of them are repetitive and stick to already known areas, each one has, in one way or the other, its own contribution to make. For example, *Chennai: Memory Chips* (Legacy Publications, Chennai) is little more than a merry-go-round for tourists, relying heavily on earlier studies. However, for all that, it is also a compendium of quaint facts that come as a pleasant surprise, especially for the long-time Madras resident.

It neatly lists landmarks, pointing out to their ancestry. Did you know that the Kapaleeswarar temple tank in Mylapore was built on land gifted by the 18th century Carnatic Nawabs? Most interesting, Muslims are permitted to come and bathe here during Moharram.

The Music College building (off Greenways Road) on the banks of the Adyar river was once the Brodie Castle. It was constructed in 1798 by an English civil servant, James Brodie. Now, after more than two hundred years, students of Carnatic music find fulfilment within its walls. Brodie himself drowned in the river in a boating accident.

The Cooum river, that ubiquitous life-line of the city which has thankfully sacrificed its much-touted stink for the sake of today's generation, is mentioned in the *Thevaram*. And Mylapore finds a reference as far back as Ptolemy in 140 A.D.

On Cathedral Road, Hotel Chola Sheraton has replaced the old house where Gandhiji once stayed. It was from here in 1910 that he announced his *satyagraha* against the Rowlatt Bill. The book contains these random little peeks behind the curtain, delighting those who know only today's Chennai.

In the city's bustle, amidst the shrill call of the IT revolution, the pubs and fashion stops, the sleek glass and upstart high-rises, it would be interesting to occasionally pause and listen to such whispers of history.

The one man who has perhaps contributed most to our knowledge of the city's past is S. Muthiah. If it isn't through his regular newspaper columns and articles, it is through an unbelievable number of books probing and celebrating the city. His stated preference is for books of the coffee-table variety with profuse illustrations and lush production values.

His books include *Madras Discovered, Tales of Old and New Madras, Madras – The Gracious City, Parrys 200, The Parry Story, Getting India on The Move, A Planting Century, Madras – its Past and its Present, The Spencer Legend, Madras – its Yesterdays and Todays and Tomorrows, At Home in Madras* and *The Spirit of Chepauk*.

His book *Madras Discovered* (164 pages) which was written in 1981 has grown in leaps and bounds, culminating for the moment in the vastly enhanced *Madras Re-discovered* (417 pages). The book has broadly everything that the armchair historian needs to know about this city, beginning with Muthiah's favourite enquiry into the origin of the city's name. He throws up stories and interesting antecedents about landmarks and events. A remarkable example of how he peels away story after story from around a single focal point can be had from the piece on Chepauk. The name is now synonymous with cricket but he talks about the Chepauk Palace which once belonged to the Nawabs of the Carnatic but ended up housing government offices. Along the way, he traces the history of the nawabs, touches upon the Madras Cricket Club and rounds off its history, adding so many more facets to the unidimensional name.

Muthiah revels in peeking behind the curtain. Preserving the heritage buildings of Madras is a holy mission for him. To achieve this, he shares his stories of the past so that even laymen can begin to understand the value of these monuments. It is no secret that many who write about the city depend on him for information. Many a heritage building has also survived because of the interest he showed in its preservation.

However, I was fortunate to bring to his notice a little-known book of fiction that threw dappled light on the city during the turn of the 19th century. This is what I wrote in my *Sunday Express* column:

'It is a novel by a woman named B.M. Croker who lived and wrote during the late 19th and early 20th centuries. The publishers have provided little information about her and the novel itself is not dated. A little bit of detective work revealed that the story takes place around 1911. The author's name rang a bell, harking back to conversations with my grandfather, and his collection of books. But I couldn't, for the life of me, place this book. It was called *In Old Madras*. And it really is. But a White Madras. The Indians are either lowly servants or faintly disreputable heads of faintly disreputable companies right in the heart of Blacktown.'

'You have a mansion in Egmore set on a vast rolling compound and of an evening there are balls and dinners and terribly focussed card games, magnificent coaches and cars driving up the impressive driveway and white sahibs and memsahibs dancing and gossiping and flirting and putting one over the other. To chill out (of course they don't say that) they drive down to the club near the Island, which must be today's Madras Gymkhana, and a beautiful-but-bored wife may leave her husband in mid-sentence in the heat of a summer evening and drive off down the promenade with an alternate escort. You have punkhas and polo and prim protocol. Mount Road, Marmalong Bridge, the Neilgherries – except for a bit of gymnastics with the spelling, they're all there and so different from how we know them today. At one point someone says, "It's in Blacktown! I beg its pardon – Georgetown!"

'I wasn't in the mood for long Jane Austenish fare. In fact, I had to grit my teeth and wade through the first few pages. And then I was coasting along. I couldn't stop! It is an exciting story. A young Englishman, Captain Mallender, newly discharged from the army, sets out to India to find the whereabouts of his uncle, missing and declared dead for the last thirty years. He thinks the man in control of his estate is now impersonating his uncle and he wants to expose him. His adventures take him to interesting places and predicaments and he meets many strange people. The Madras we find in the book is a fascinating place of slow boulevards and leisurely life-styles. (Of course, you would have to be white and British.)

'There is intrigue and deception, romance and love, excitement and adventure, physical pain and heartbreak. The ending is breath-stopping. The hero travels incognito and you are as tense as he is when he chances upon unexpected discoveries. When he arrives at a place named Panjeverram, I couldn't help but exclaim: "Good Lord, are you talking about Kancheepuram, or have you misspelled some other name!"

'It's been a long time since I have read such a book. Robust and romantic and frankly unputdownable. It has its clichés and melodrama and pat situations, but what is life without those! And incidentally it gave me plenty of information about Madras in that sepia-tinted time. Madras according to Croker, that is' (9 March 2003, *New Indian Express*).

Muthiah was so taken up by the reference that he immediately bought and read the book and discussed it at a Madras Book Club meeting. He found several holes in its authenticity, especially with regard to dates, but thoroughly enjoyed the spirit of the place it conjured up.

I would also like to make a passing reference to another book compiled towards the middle of the last century. *History Of The World*, edited by W.N. Weech and published by Odhams Press, London, is only relevant here for its brief conjecture about the quality of the Tamils. It probably explains the abundance of culture and trade, and the inward-looking native trait that discounted any ideas of expansionism: 'The Tamil and Telugu states in the south, especially those on the coasts of Travancore and Madras, were rich and prosperous, and Tamil poets flourished. Their sailors took their cargoes of cotton to the Ganges and the Irrawaddy. But their soldiers were never formidable and, though boundaries shifted, no southern ruler ever looked like uniting India.'

And continuing with references to Madras, here are some extracts from *Introduction to India* by Toby Sinclair (Odyssey Guides,

Hong Kong, 1991). 'Despite its size and importance, Madras is a city that never hurries. Compared with India's other major cities, Madras is a quiet backwater, conservative in its ways, with considerable importance placed on old-fashioned values and traditions. More women wear the traditional sari here than anywhere else in India; Brahmin men in finely woven white dhotis, their foreheads smeared with sandalpaste and sacred ash, go happily about their business, and every woman, regardless of status, has flowers in her hair.

'For all this, Madras is a clean and efficient city. It has an excellent public transport system; its autorickshaw scooters are all new and well maintained... There are some unexpected contrasts: the garish Tamil film posters decorating sections of Mount Road; the massive cutouts of politicians; and the hysteria of political meetings are just a few. Although Madras presents fewer of the hassles and tensions common in other Indian cities, the main shopping centres are always throbbing with life... The people of Madras smile easily, have time for each other and are helpful to visitors.'

I had, for a long time, been looking out for a novel in English and set in Madras, written by a Tamilian named S. Y. Krishnaswamy. A grand-uncle had once certified that it provided an authentic portrait of the city of its time. It was called *Kalyani's Husband*. There was a film of the same name, starring Sivaji Ganesan, and I wasn't sure whether it was an adaptation of this novel. Surfing the net to locate the book, I came across several Kalyanis and their husbands, but not the ones I wanted. When I entrusted the job to my son, he effortlessly and triumphantly returned with the book, having found it among a cache of old retrieved tomes.

The author, in his introduction, claims that the story is based on the life of his cousin Kalyani and his friend Sekhar. He isn't writing fiction but 'about those who have been near and dear to me.' He says his job is easy because he doesn't have to invent, but difficult 'because I have to betray confidences without consent.' He is torn between the 'surging flood of recollection straining at my reticence' and his natural reluctance to wear his heart on his sleeve. He goes on to write that English novels of Indian life are 'poor stuff'. Nevertheless, he has decided to 'take the plunge'.

The language and manner of writing reminds you of a Hardy or Austen in spate. The novel begins in the grand manner with a stretched-out description of Madras ('there are changes of fashion in a city, as in women's clothes, but not of the same order of rapidity'). He describes people (merchant princes in their finery and the judges and leaders of the bar) and places (the commercial north and the more intellectual south). He is lavish about Mylapore, which he likens to Manchester. 'What Mylapore thought today Madras thinks tomorrow.' He devotes over five pages to this description, and never looks back throughout the novel. His descriptions are often tedious but follow the literary fashion of the day. He takes time to expand on various themes, intellectualising and philosophising, and even dwells at length on the intricacies of South Indian vegetarian cuisine.

Kalyani's Husband is mostly light and descriptive, and is easily a tale of manners, though its hero dies at the end of the story. That the author is smitten by Victorian novels is obvious, and Madras takes the place of London. The novel was printed at the Huntley Press, Armenian Street, in 1957.

A name that keeps haunting you as you go about hunting material on the city is that of Randor Guy. He is a former lawyer named Rangadurai who uses his pen-name to intrigue readers into a world of whispered gossip and torrid romance, all from the bygone glitter of Madras. His chief playing field is cinema. There is little that he hasn't discovered about the triumphs and tragedies of yesteryear heroes and heroines of the Tamil silver screen. He has a phenomenal memory which assists him as much during his lectures as when he is writing. It is through these lectures and his articles and columns that he shares his often shocking stories. One of these stories is about a rich and famous gentleman of the city who was fond of playing Krishna. Armed with a flute and a mischievous smile, he sat atop a tree as scantily-clad girls hired for the purpose pleaded for their clothes from his swimming pool. Guy's 'history' of Madras is peppered with such almost unbelievable tales of drama and glitter.

His tales are peopled with legends like M.S. Subbulakshmi, Thyagaraja Bhagavathar, S.S. Vasan, MGR and a host of such unforgettable names. Already brimming with nostalgia, Guy further embellishes these names with his forays into a secret past.

The Story Of Fort St. George by Col. D.M. Reid, printed two years before independence at the Diocesan Press, has a foreword by the Madras Governor, Sir Arthur Hope. It was reissued in 1999 by Asian Educational Services (AES) in a trademark purple and gold edition. It is a small book, tracing the story of how the Fort was conceived and executed. Starting from Francis Day's appeal to his superior Andrew Cogan to grab the opportunity and start work on a settlement at the site that he had negotiated for, to a grand tour of the Fort as it was during his time. He narrates the history of European interest in the area and how the British clinched their claim. There is a chronological table of events and illustrations showing the progressive changes in the premises. It is a brief study, focusing on the Fort and its historical background, adding to the numerous works on the city's founding. The (short-lived) pride of the Englishman is evident throughout the book.

Another Englishman with a penchant for Chennai is Colin Todhunter. Reading more like a diary of his escapades in a hot and mystic land, *Chasing Rainbows in Chennai* (published by Hacktreks, Canada, and marketed by Zine5, Chennai) has been of late discussed and read at quite a few venues. It is a mixture of pained and amused observation that brings to life the small details of daily living that escape the average citizen. He begins with an arduous trip to a gym where 'personality' is more vital than any tedious workout. It sets the stage for a 100 odd-page saga of helplessness, discovery and acutely felt experience.

He has a wild two-wheeler trip to Pondicherry, a painfully one-sided love affair, and many encounters with fellow travellers with weird identity problems; he acts in a film, ponders on the mysteries of train travel and the ubiquitous vendor, he enjoys 'meals' in roadside restaurants and philosophises on almost everything he sees. It doesn't help that he bears a strong resemblance to the Mumbai film star Sanjay Dutt. I met Colin in the beginning of last year. He was steeped in Chennai. It was a love-hate relationship that made him flee the city and then scamper back in no time at all.

These and many more raconteurs have sung about Madras that is Chennai. It isn't over as yet. The layers are still being peeled away as story after fascinating story emerges, still waiting to lay bare the longed-for, elusive soul of the city.